338.4

CAREERS WITHOUT COLLEGE

TRAVEL

by Robert F. Miller

Series developed by Peggy Schmidt

Peterson's

Princeton, New Jersey

A New Century Communications Book

Other titles in

this series include:

CARS

COMPUTERS

EMERGENCIES

FASHION

FITNESS

HEALTH CARE

KIDS

MUSIC

SPORTS

Library of Congress Cataloging-in-Publication Data

Miller, Robert F. (Robert Finch), 1944–
    Travel / by Robert F. Miller.
        p.   cm.—(Careers without college)
    "A New Century Communications book."
    Summary: Describes five jobs in the world of travel (travel agent, flight attendant, reservations agent, customer service agent, tour manager), none of which requires a college degree, and discusses the skills needed to do them, their advantages and disadvantages, and their growth potential.
    ISBN 1-56079-249-3 (pbk.) : $7.95
    1. Tourist trade—Vocational guidance.   [1. Tourist trade—Vocational guidance.
2. Vocational guidance.]   I. Title.   II. Series.
G155.5.M54   1993
338.4'791'023—dc20   93-4638
                                                                                                             CIP
                                                                                                              AC

Art direction: Linda Huber
Cover photo: Bryce Flynn Photography
Cover and interior design: Greg Wozney Design, Inc.
Composition: Bookworks Plus
Printed in the United States of America
10 9 8 7 6 5 4 3 2 1

Text Photo Credits
Color photo graphics: J. Gerard Smith Photography
Page xiv: © Photo Edit/Michael Newman
Page 18: © The Stock Market/Ted Horowitz
Page 36: © The Bettman Archive
Page 54: © The Stock Market/Don Mason
Page 72: © Photo Edit/Michael Newman

ABOUT THIS SERIES

Careers without College is designed to help those who don't have a four-year college degree (and don't plan on getting one any time soon) find a career that fits their interests, talents and personality. It's for you if you're about to choose your career—or if you're planning to change careers and don't want to invest a lot of time or money in more education or training, at least not right at the start.

Some of the jobs featured do require an associate degree; others only require on-the-job training that may take a year, some months or only a few weeks. In today's increasingly competitive job market, you may want to eventually consider getting a two- or maybe a four-year college degree in order to move up in a field.

Each title in the series features five jobs in a particular industry or career area. Some of them are "ordinary," others are glamorous. The competition to get into certain featured occupations is intense; as a balance, we have selected jobs under the same career umbrella that are easier to enter. Some of the other job opportunities within each field will be featured in future titles in this series.

Careers without College has up-to-date information that comes from extensive interviews with experts in each field. The format of each book is designed for easy reading. Plus, each book gives you something unique: an insider's look at the featured jobs through interviews with people who work in them now.

We invite your comments about the series, which will help us with future titles. Please send your correspondence to: Careers without College, c/o Peterson's Guides, Inc., P.O. Box 2123, Princeton, NJ 08543-2123.

Peggy Schmidt has written about education and careers for 20 years. She is author of Peterson's best-selling *The 90-Minute Resume*.

ACKNOWLEDGMENTS

Many thanks to the following people for their invaluable assistance in the preparation of this book:

Edwina Arnold, Public Relations Director, Club Med, New York, New York

Aly Bello, Public Relations Coordinator, Carnival Cruise Line, Miami, Florida

Ted Bravos, Director, ITMI, San Francisco, California

Judi Bredemeier, Washington Correspondent, CMP Publications, Fairfax, Virginia

Barbara Brooks, Senior Account Supervisor, M. Silver Associates, New York, New York

Lynn Cutter, Vice President, Marketing, Special Expeditions, New York, New York

Randy Durband, Managing Director, Resources, Tauck Tours, Westport, Connecticut

Justin Ferate, Tour Services Director, Grayline Tours, New York, New York

Heidi Fritz, Tour Coordinator, Globus Cosmos Tourama, Pasadena, California

Larry Frommer, President, Frommer Travel Designers, Washington, D.C.

Jim Glab, author, New York, New York

Ray Greenley, Vice President, Consumer Affairs, American Society of Travel Agents, Alexandria, Virginia

Larry Flowe, Flight Attendant Supervisor, USAir, Charlotte, North Carolina

Linnea Smith Jessup, President, Smith Jessup Communications, Walnut Creek, California

Lori Levin, Director, Public Relations, Virgin Atlantic, New York, New York

Lynette Hinings Marshall, President, International Guide Academy, Denver, Colorado

Kathleen Lingle Pond, author, Northern Virginia Community College, Charlottesville, Virginia

Anne Marie Powell, Vice President, Marketing, Alamo Rent-A-Car, Fort Lauderdale, Florida

Bill Price, Manager, Inflight Services, Tower Air, New York, New York

Barry Robinson, Flight Operations Manager, American Airlines, New York, New York

Kathy Sudeikis, Vice President, Brennco Travel, Kansas City, Missouri

Dale Vestal, Director, Tour Management, Maupintour, Inc., Lawrence, Kansas

Brendan Viera, Reservations Supervisor, Cunard Line, New York, New York

WHAT'S IN THIS BOOK

WHY THESE TRAVEL CAREERS?

The travel and tourism industry accounts for more than $3 trillion in global spending every year and employs about one out of every ten workers in the world.

This book focuses on five of the most important jobs in travel and tourism, none of which requires a four-year education. What's more important is to be able to handle customers effectively over the phone and in person—skills you can develop quickly in any job that requires dealing with the public. The five jobs are:

- ❏ Travel agent
- ❏ Flight attendant
- ❏ Reservations agent
- ❏ Customer service agent
- ❏ Tour manager

The work of these travel industry employees is essential to the operations of the industry because it is through them that reservations are made, travel products and services are sold, customer problems are solved and tours are conducted. Some jobs are found in every segment of the industry; every kind of travel company needs reservations and customer service agents, for example. While tour managers work primarily for tour operators, they sometimes work for travel agents, cruise lines and airlines.

Each of these careers is unique in character and function and will appeal to different interests. And each demands particular skills and talents.

Some 250,000 travel agents arrange travel and vacations to all parts of the world for individuals and groups. Over 100,000 flight attendants help ensure that air travel is safe and enjoyable. The thousands of reservations agents and customer service agents are the vital link between the public and the travel product; without them there wouldn't be a ticket sold or a question answered. And tour managers may be local sightseeing experts or escorts for groups of travelers to places as distant as China, Japan and Hong Kong.

The glamour, mystery and excitement that make travel such a wonderful and rewarding part of everyone's life are among the big benefits for the people who work in the travel industry. Flight attendants zip off to ski in the European Alps with regularity; tour escorts are wined and dined in the most expensive hotels at someone else's expense. Travel agents explore the islands of the South Pacific courtesy of airlines, hotels and tour companies.

Working in the field of travel is hard work, and it's often repetitive and routine. At times it means keeping a smile on your face while dealing with difficult, demanding strangers. Or it may mean working on Christmas when you're miles from home. And it often takes the wonderful benefits of free travel to the places you've always dreamed about to make up for salaries that won't make you rich.

On the other hand, there is no industry in the world with better opportunities for the person with ambition, energy and the spirit of adventure. Travel and tourism is an industry where a good idea coupled with confidence can take you places. For the person who is willing to work hard and learn the ropes, the jobs in this book can help launch a highly rewarding career.

ROBERT H. DICKINSON

on Why Travel is a Hot Career Ticket

It may be only a slight exaggeration to say that Bob Dickinson created today's vacation business. He's certainly the reason that some 20,000 people every week sail off on cruises to the Caribbean, the Gulf of Mexico or the Bahamas. And that's just the people sailing on the ships of Carnival Cruise Lines, where Dickinson is senior vice president of sales and marketing.

Carnival is the world's most successful cruise company, perhaps even the most successful travel company of any kind. More than a million people take a vacation on a Carnival ship every year. Before Carnival, cruises were for the elderly and rich; now they're for every secretary, office manager, lawyer, family and honeymoon couple. Dickinson's success as the company's supersalesman has changed the way every travel company in the industry sells its product. And in a business where the movers and shakers are usually working too hard to gain much stardom, Dickinson has managed to sell the world on "fun" and become a celebrity in the travel industry.

When he joined Carnival, Dickinson's assignment was to get rid of a failing, unknown company. "We were the bottom feeders of the industry," he says. Instead, he turned the company around by reinventing the concept of cruising and revolutionizing the cruise industry. Now Carnival has a fleet of nine ships, six of them brand new, and another four on the way, each of which cost more than $300 million! Carnival Cruise Lines also owns two subsidiary companies, Holland America Cruises and Windstar Cruises, and has a 25 percent interest in Seabourn Cruise Lines. Almost every travel agent who sells cruises has heard Dickinson speak, has met him personally or at least knows his name. And most TV viewers have seen Kathie Lee Gifford's commercials for the "fun" ships of Carnival.

Dickinson's efforts in promoting vacation travel have earned him Travel Person of the Year honors and chairmanship of the Cruise Lines International Association, and he is also incoming chairman of the Travel Industry Association. Here are his thoughts about why you should consider going into the travel industry.

Tourism is one of the fastest growing areas of the national and international economies. And there's a very good reason: Unlike other things that people buy, there's no limit to the amount of travel or vacationing you can do. Unless you're Andre Agassi, how many tennis rackets can you have? How many golf clubs do you need? Travel is something you can do again and again—there's no end to it.

Everybody's talking about the "global village"—how the world is getting smaller as communications get better. But what's really making the world a village is the fact that people are traveling in larger and larger numbers. What this means for a young person starting a career today is that there is a tremendous future ahead in travel and tourism. Who knows—toward the end of your career, you may be traveling in outer space!

The most rewarding aspect of this industry for me is that we sell happiness. Consumers fight the rat race for 50 weeks a year and then they take a week, two weeks off. When they travel they rest, relax and have fun. And there's something about making that possible for someone, about being a provider of vacations, that's very gratifying. You're giving people something they look forward to, something they've saved for. Even for the thousands of people involved in more routine kinds of travel such as arranging travel for businesspeople or operating computers and reservations systems for the airlines, there is the satisfaction that comes from knowing you've provided a useful, often essential service for someone. These kinds of jobs make you feel good at the end of the day.

Then there's the diversity of the travel industry. From travel agents to cruise staff to airline personnel and tour managers, there are all kinds of jobs to be done and a whole range of challenges to meet. Some people do operational jobs; they keep the tours running smoothly or handle reservations. Others, such as flight attendants or customer service agents, deal with the public. Still others are in sales and marketing.

The biggest challenge for those of us in the cruise business is persuading people to choose a cruise for their vacation. Only six percent of the American public have ever been on a cruise. So we're trying to tell the other 94 percent about an experience they know nothing about. We're not only trying to tell them about it and have them understand what fun it is, we're trying to convince them to buy into the experience. That's a pretty tough job.

The tourism industry's variety has another benefit for people working in it. You can start out working for an airline and through working in that industry end up in the hotel side of the business or with a rent-a-car company or a

cruise line. In other words, just because you start out in
one sector you don't necessarily have to end up there.
That's not as true in most other industries. The advantage
is that it gives you more career options, and the more options there are, the better chance you have of advancing
your career.

The career opportunities for people starting out in travel
and tourism are excellent. In our company, for example,
we have 275 entry-level positions for which college degrees
are not required. There are positions available in all sectors
of the industry, whether they're for flight attendants or
rent-a-car reservations agents or cruise staff. In fact, the
industry is full of people holding very responsible jobs who
didn't need a four-year degree to enter the business. Some
of our most successful salesmen and women around the
country didn't go to college, including my wife. She was
one of Carnival's top salespeople, and before she worked
with us she was a part owner of four travel agencies. A
sizable percentage of the 250,000 travel agents in North
America have created very successful careers without college degrees.

What we are seeing more and more of, though, are
people with a two-year associate degree, and many of those
people are apt to go on and finish a four-year program
eventually. The other interesting trend is that a lot of high
schools these days are graduating people who are very computer literate. Because the travel industry has become
highly computerized in the last ten years, people who are
knowledgeable about computers are entering the industry
in relatively advanced-level jobs with just a high school
degree. These are jobs that would not ordinarily be open to
people who are 18 years old.

Essentially, what we in the travel industry look for
when hiring are "hospitality" people: people who are
friendly and warm and service-oriented, who have a head
on their shoulders. A certain amount of street smarts also
helps, but the bottom line is that we want people who have
common sense, focus and discipline.

There are two basic kinds of personalities in this industry, often called "back of the house" and "front of the
house." Front of the house people are personable and outgoing; they put other people at ease. They can look you

directly in the eye when they're talking to you, and they make you feel warm and welcome.

Front of the house jobs generally are the ones involved with the customer; these are the people who work in airports, for car rental companies or on cruise ships. They might be travel agents working in a busy shopping mall or sales representatives who work for airlines, cruise lines or tour operators. What the front of the house people have in common is that their job involves working with the public, whether it's one-on-one travel consulting or escorting a tour group or working with 2,600 cruise passengers.

Back of the house people are equally important in the business. Their personalities may be quieter, and they may not enjoy meeting the public as much and prefer to work in a relative degree of isolation. These people are very results-oriented, very disciplined and very organized.

Back of the house people are the ones who are best at operations; they're people who usually handle reservations and computer systems, who make sure we've got the right number of rooms for the people who are signed up or who handle travel arrangements for businesspeople. Very often they have little contact with people other than their fellow workers.

What all this adds up to, I think, is that a career in travel and tourism can be anything you want to make it. This is an industry where spirit and determination count more than putting in your time with a huge company. Travel agents go on to be travel agency owners; reservation agents become top sales representatives. That's what makes it all so challenging and so rewarding. If you've got the drive and the discipline, if you're good at working hard without supervision, and if you have imagination, there's a real chance to write your own ticket to success.

FAMOUS BEGINNINGS

Phillip Gordon, Managing Director of Planning and Operations for Globus & Cosmos Tourama, the world's largest tour company

Gordon was a part-time tour guide throughout high school and had decided to go to college. The lure of good pay and lots of travel persuaded him to work full time as a tour guide instead. After leading and planning tours for Globus in Italy and Switzerland, he helped launch his company's Visit USA tours and ended up in America. He now plans trips for tens of thousands of people to the most popular cities and to the most remote wilderness areas throughout North America and the Pacific region.

Maryles Casto, Owner, Casto Travel, one of the largest privately owned travel agencies in the United States

Casto started in the industry as a flight attendant. She then went to work for a travel agency, where she felt her efforts were unrewarded. She was also frustrated by the agency's inflexibility toward working mothers. As a result, she decided to create her own job. She started Casto Travel in San Francisco with $3,000. It was named to *Savvy* magazine's Top 60 list of businesses owned by women in 1992. Casto is the only woman to have received the Asian Pacific American Heritage Award from President George Bush.

Richard Branson, Founder of Virgin Atlantic Airways and the Voyager Group

Branson made his first million at age 17 by publishing a magazine for young British people. After creating the successful entertainment company Virgin Records, he launched a plan to revolutionize air travel by offering first class service at bargain prices. Then he founded Virgin Holidays, a company that takes 150,000 people a year on package vacations. In his spare time Branson set the speed record for crossing the Atlantic Ocean by speedboat and was copilot on the first hot air balloon crossings of the Atlantic and the Pacific.

Are you an armchair traveler—someone who loves to read about distant places or experience the world through *National Geographic* specials? Do you enjoy planning the details of vacations? Is exploring a new place the kind of experience that challenges and excites you? If few subjects interest you more than travel and you're great with details, becoming a travel agent may be your passport to real job satisfaction.

Travel agents plan and arrange travel—they get you on the airplane, find you a hotel or book you on a tour. Using computers, telephones and price lists, they can find the least expensive airfare or the most exclusive resort for their clients, who may be corporations, schools, groups or business or leisure travelers.

1

Their job is to take the stress and hassle out of travel. Research may involve hours on the computer or on the telephone talking to airlines, hotels and wholesalers (who put together tour packages). Good travel agents are sticklers for detail and keep records of everything they learn or do. The smallest mistake in a fare or schedule can mean inconvenience, even catastrophe, for the traveler.

To succeed as a travel agent, you have to be patient and not easily ruffled by the people at the airlines, hotels and car rental companies who supply information. They may not always be prompt in getting back to you, or they may put you on hold for long periods. And you must be persistent and thorough in tracking down the most up-to-date information and prices.

A travel agent has to be able to get along with all kinds of people. A good agent also knows how to come to the rescue when things go wrong.

And things often do go wrong—flights get delayed or canceled, hotel room reservations are "lost," unannounced changes are made in tour itineraries. Even when the weather, mechanical difficulties, a computer failure or human error is the cause, the travel agent is the one who hears about it and—when possible—has to remedy the problem. The best agents are those who can listen and do their best to come up with an alternative or soothe the client without getting upset themselves.

Even though you'll be dealing with travel day in and day out, don't expect to be a globetrotter yourself—at least not overnight. Travel agents do get discounts on airlines, cruises, hotels and tours, but usually after they have been working at least a year. There are also familiarization or "fam" trips offered for low prices by airlines, tourist bureaus, hotels and tour companies. While more experienced agents often get first crack at these trips, some agencies encourage new employees to participate, believing it's important for them to become acquainted with hotels, resorts and destinations.

If you enjoy meeting and working with new people, are good at organizing and planning and can handle the pressure of getting answers or finding solutions in what might be a tight time frame, you are likely to find success as a travel agent.

What You Need to Know

- ❑ Airline and other computer reservations systems—helpful but not essential
- ❑ Basic retail sales techniques
- ❑ Basic math (so you can easily add up costs)
- ❑ World geography

Necessary Skills

- ❑ Good listening skills (so you know exactly what clients and suppliers want)
- ❑ Ability to communicate information accurately
- ❑ Good note-taking and record-keeping skills
- ❑ Ability to access and use reference materials quickly
- ❑ Ability to ask the right questions of clients and suppliers
- ❑ Foreign language fluency—useful but not essential
- ❑ Talent for organizing your work and work day
- ❑ A pleasant telephone manner

Do You Have What It Takes?

- ❑ Ability to work independently
- ❑ Self-confidence to inspire the trust of would-be clients
- ❑ Sensitivity to clients' needs and personalities
- ❑ Ability to handle complaints without losing your cool
- ❑ Patience, which comes in handy when customers can't make up their minds or have no patience themselves
- ❑ Punctuality (especially important in a small agency)
- ❑ Ability to take direction (from agency managers)
- ❑ Persistence (information isn't always easy to get)
- ❑ Ability to network and get new clients

Physical Requirements

- ❑ A well-groomed appearance

Education

No specific courses or degrees are required, but an understanding of how computers work is essential (you will receive on-the-job training on your agency's specific computer systems when you start work).

Licenses Required

The only state that requires licensing is Rhode Island, which requires agents to pass a test of 100 questions covering general knowledge of the travel industry. The test may be taken after you are hired as an apprentice agent.

Job Outlook

Job opportunities: very good

Jobs are plentiful—the travel agency business is one of the fastest-growing industries because technological advances in communications and transportation are making travel available and affordable to more people and businesses. There has been a 40 percent increase in the number of travel agencies since 1980. One of the hottest trends is the growth of special interest agencies—companies specializing in one kind of travel (such as bicycle trips or barge cruises) or catering to certain groups (families with young children, senior citizens or singles). Much faster than average employment growth for travels agents is projected through the 1990s.

The Ground Floor

Entry-level jobs: Receptionist, reservationist (taking and processing travel requests), computer operator (processing data and ticket requests), assistant (to a more experienced agent)

On-the-Job Responsibilities

Beginners

❑ Greet and direct customers to experienced agents
❑ Answer telephones and direct calls
❑ Handle mailing, display and reordering of agency's brochures and promotional information

❏ Input travel data on automated reservations system
❏ Take simple orders or travel requests from customers
❏ Assist more experienced agents in planning trips for individuals or groups
❏ Issue tickets using the automated reservations system

Experienced Travel Agents

In addition to some of the above:

❏ Research travel destinations by consulting books, maps and computer data bases
❏ Provide travel advice and information to clients
❏ Plan itineraries and make reservations for travel, hotels, car rentals, cruises and tour packages by computer and telephone
❏ Work with travel departments in corporations to make travel arrangements for business clients
❏ Work with meeting planners to arrange travel for meetings and conferences
❏ Help obtain visas and passports (get forms for clients and help file them)
❏ Sell travel insurance
❏ Go on familiarization (fam) trips to inspect hotels and attractions
❏ Supervise other employees and train new agents
❏ Attend industry meetings
❏ Participate in industry trade associations

Travel agents typically work 40-hour-plus weeks. The length of a day depends on how effectively you work: paperwork, record-keeping and ticketing must often be completed immediately rather than left for the next day.

Busy periods depend on the kind of business the agency does. If the agency primarily deals with pleasure or vacation travel, the periods leading up to major holidays, school holidays and the summer vacation period are the most active. If its clientele is primarily business travelers, the longest days will come when your clients have major meetings or conferences.

◆ **When You'll Work**

Time Off
◆ In your first year, you'll generally get one or two weeks of vacation time, plus the major holidays (Christmas, Thanksgiving, Fourth of July). You may, however, end up working on some holidays, even federal ones such as President's Day.

Perks
◆
- ❏ Fam trips
- ❏ Discounts on travel (travel agents generally receive up to 75 percent discounts on travel and accommodations)
- ❏ Free promotional items such as tee shirts
- ❏ Health and life insurance (about 30 percent of agencies cover health insurance premiums; 60 percent contribute to life insurance policies)

Who's Hiring
◆
- ❏ Retail travel agencies (vacation and business travel)
- ❏ Corporate travel agencies (only business travel)
- ❏ Cruise-only agencies
- ❏ Agencies catering to special interest groups
- ❏ Banks (a growing number now offer travel services)
- ❏ Universities (travel programs for students and alumni)
- ❏ Associations or organizations such as museums, non-profit groups or cultural foundations that offer travel programs to their members

On-the-Job Hazards
◆
- ❏ Carpal tunnel syndrome (a wrist injury that can occur from using a computer keyboard for hours every day)
- ❏ Lower back strain (from hours of sitting without adequate back support)
- ❏ Stress-related problems brought on by work pace and demands from clients
- ❏ Eyestrain and headaches (from staring at a computer screen for hours)

Beginners: limited travel opportunities

Experienced travel agents: great travel opportunities

Some agencies (often larger ones) encourage new travel agents to take fam trips as part of their training. Smaller agencies have a more difficult time giving new agents the time off to do so. Opportunities come with seniority or because of the type of work you do in the agency. If you specialize in foreign or vacation travel, you are apt to take more fam trips because you need to be familiar with destinations in order to recommend them.

All travel agents affiliated with an accredited travel agency are entitled to discounts offered by airlines, cruise lines, hotels and other travel suppliers.

◆ **Places You'll Go**

Travel agencies can be found anywhere from a shopping mall to a skyscraper to a stand-alone building, so offices vary in character. The storefront variety sport big windows filled with posters and models of planes. Corporate travel departments have the same character as other offices in that company.

Whatever the location or decor, there is usually little privacy. Desks are adjacent to one another, and you can overhear others' conversations. Clients are often directed to seats opposite your desk, which means that people are watching and listening as you work. The sound of ringing telephones, clicking keyboards and printers at work can be a low roar.

In agencies dealing with corporate travel, business is conducted by telephone and you rarely see the client.

◆ **Surroundings**

Starting salaries: $12,000-$17,000

Five years experience: $17,000-$25,000

Top earners: $25,000-$32,000 (excluding managers and owners)

Most travel agents earn a straight salary. Agencies in major metropolitan areas and large agencies that specialize in corporate travel pay more. Many agencies, however, offer bonuses based on sales or excellence of service to

◆ **Dollars and Cents**

their customers.

It's possible to earn commissions if you are affiliated with an agency as an outside sales representative and cover your own office expenses.

Moving Up

After apprenticing and proving you've got what it takes, you can become a full-fledged travel agent. In all but the smallest agencies, agents tend to focus on pleasure or business travel. In larger agencies, you might narrow your focus even further, specializing in foreign travel, group travel or cruises.

The key to advancement is performance: how well you handle clients, whether they keep coming back to you, how efficiently you do your work and how enthusiastic you are. In a small agency, you could be named a manager after 5 years experience; in a large agency, it might take you 15 years.

Because most agencies are small, you often have a better chance of being promoted if you jump from agency to agency, which is acceptable.

Where the Jobs Are

About half of the agencies in the United States are in the suburbs; another 40 percent can be found in cities, and the remaining 10 percent service small town populations. Most agencies that specialize in business travel are located in major metropolitan areas.

The Male/Female Equation

The large majority of travel agents are women, but more men are going into the field. The prospect of owning their own agency has attracted more men, and it has resulted in more women than ever owning their own businesses and providing leadership in the industry.

The Bad News

❏ Lots of paperwork
❏ Difficult or demanding customers
❏ You'll be glued to your desk, headset and computer monitor
❏ Pressure to stay on top of changing information
❏ Lack of control over problems that affect clients

The Good News

❏ Opportunity to travel inexpensively
❏ Grateful customers
❏ Plentiful job openings
❏ Good training for those who want their own agency
❏ No two days are ever alike

◆ **Making Your Decision: What to Consider**

◆ **Training**

A number of high schools, community colleges and for-profit travel schools offer courses that can be helpful, but are not essential, in landing a job. Most travel agents get their training on the job. Some agencies send new employees to schools operated by airlines to learn the automated reservations systems (SABRE and PARS are two of the biggest ones) that are used to book airline reservations.

The American Society of Travel Agents (ASTA) offers a home study course and administers a three-hour test; those who pass earn a Certificate of Proficiency. An 18-month part-time study curriculum is offered by the Institute of Certified Travel Agents and entitles you to call yourself a Certified Travel Counselor. A large percentage of managers and owners are ICTA graduates.

WHAT IT'S REALLY LIKE

Darryl Tsukuda, 22,
travel agent, Zenith Travel,
New York, New York
Years in travel: four

How did you get started in the travel business?
I started as a travel agent right out of high school. I got a
job working for a 24-hour travel service. We had two weeks
of on-the-job training, and from there they put us right on
the phones handling clients. I did all I could possibly do to
learn everything quickly. The first step was learning all the
major computer reservation systems to make bookings with
the airlines and hotels.

What was the hardest part?
One problem was the hours. Because it was a 24-hour
agency, I worked at all times of the day and night. I knew
the computers and a little bit about how the travel industry
worked, but I had to learn everything else on the job—how
to respond to questions I didn't expect and give the best
possible answers over the phone. It sure was a rapid learning process.

What's your current job like?
I work as a corporate travel agent for Zenith Travel in New

York, servicing Elizabeth Arden. We arrange air travel, rail travel, hotel accommodations and car rental reservations for its employees on business all over the world. We also work as meeting planners to arrange all the details and bookings for corporate meetings and conferences. Basically, we work from 9 to 5:30, taking calls from corporate clients and making reservations via computer.

What do you like best about it?
What I like most about being a travel agent is that I get to travel. I've been an agent for four years, and I've already been to Europe, including Spain, France and Germany, and I've seen most of the United States. I've taken cruises on five-star ships and gone to islands in the Caribbean. Some of it has been on fam trips, but most was just taking advantage of the free travel we get as agents.

I also like what I'm doing and get great satisfaction from the job itself. I enjoy the one-to-one contact with clients. I don't think this is what I want to do for the rest of my travel career, though. I'd like to move up the ladder and get an executive position. I might not be working as closely with the clients, but I would be generating revenue for the company, maybe working as a sales agent landing new business accounts or in some other capacity. But in the meantime, I'm very happy with what I'm doing.

What don't you like about the job?
What I like least, I guess, are the hours. We're supposed to work from 9 to 5:30, but sometimes it's 9 to 8:30— whatever it takes to get the job done for the client. But that's really my only complaint. I work with some pretty nice people, and the clients are nice. The clients who aren't? I don't let them get to me. I go on to the next one.

Do you think there's a certain type of person who makes the best travel agent?
I don't think there's any one personality type that makes a good travel agent because it's a learned skill. Some days you may not feel like being nice and helpful, but that's the job. And that's something you won't learn in the first year or maybe even the second year in this business. But eventually you learn how to deal with clients and with your co-workers; you learn it as you go along.

What's your advice to someone interested in being a travel agent?

I know there are a lot of travel schools out there, and many people would probably advise getting some travel industry education before looking for a job. But I'm against it because I know people who have gone to travel schools and haven't been able to do anything with that education. It might be useful to have some background, but it's still going to get down to on-the-job training like I had, I think.

I'd advise someone looking for a job as a travel agent to present himself or herself as confidently as possible. That's the key to getting your foot in the door. Then learn as much as you can on the job. Try to gain a customer service orientation—the whole job is getting along with the customers and making the arrangements they need. Be as confident as you can when talking to clients—let them know that you know what you're doing, because then you gain their trust. Finally, I'd advise being open to criticism, because when you're green, you're green, and everybody has to learn the ropes.

Helen Rousso, 25,
travel agent, Tzell Travel,
East Norwich, New York
Years in travel: seven

How did you get started in the travel business?

I was working for an insurance broker and was bored to death. I'd always wanted to get into the travel field. I guess I got in by luck: A friend of mine was offered a position with an agency, but she already had a job, so I went in to see the agency. The people liked me and were willing to give me on-the-job training.

What was the hardest part of your job in the beginning?

My first day on the job was pretty scary. It was a small agency, and when the boss went out at lunchtime, someone called up to make a reservation. I didn't even know how to go about it; nobody had told me anything yet! Getting started without any training was the hardest thing. I had to learn quickly how to make a reservation and figure out all the different airfares, using the city codes the airlines require.

I've never gone through a travel agency-type training course, but I have learned all the different computer reservations systems. Usually, your employer will send you to one of the training schools the airlines set up to teach people their automated ticketing systems.

What's your current job like?

Another girl and I head up the corporate department of this travel agency. That means we arrange business travel for several corporations, but we also handle a lot of leisure, or vacation, travel. We make reservations, issue tickets, sell vacation packages and cruises and plan individual trips. It's a lot of research, and you need to know where to find the information necessary to make the arrangements and make recommendations to the customer. I don't think any school can really teach you that; you just have to learn to do the research on the job.

What do you like best about the job?

There's a difference between what I like and what's the easiest to do. Arranging travel for businesspeople is the easiest because it's usually just booking flights, hotels and car rentals in places they have to go. What I get the most satisfaction from are the vacation trips I plan. I love doing the work to find out where the best places are for each client. It's a matter of matching what I know about my customer with what I know about travel destinations and then recommending the right trip—finding just the right little hideaway for the right person. And I'll say this: When you make all those arrangements and the client comes home a happy traveler, you feel terrific!

I also like the people in this business. As a travel agent you have to enjoy working with people; if you're not a people person you're not going to do well.

What is your biggest dislike?

Difficult clients. People who are unpleasant aren't fun to work with, but even worse are clients who won't give me any information beyond "Send me someplace warm."

That's the travel agent's nightmare. The more details you have, the easier your job is, and that may mean spending hours on the phone with a client.

Have you done a lot of traveling yourself?
The travel benefits are one reward that makes all the more unpleasant parts of the job acceptable. I've been on fam trips and have taken advantage of discounts that are available to travel agents. I've been to Israel and Europe and to some of the islands in the Caribbean. St. Barts is beautiful! And I've been to Mexico and all over the U.S., including Florida, California and Washington, D.C.

Do you think there's a certain type of person who makes the best agent?
There are all kinds of people working as travel agents. You definitely have to be personable; the people you deal with have to trust you and like you so they'll take your advice. And you have to be patient. If you can't handle people who change their plans every hour, keep you waiting or make crazy requests, then being a travel agent is definitely not for you.

What's your advice to someone interested in being a travel agent?
I'd say prepare yourself as best you can. Read the travel magazines and the travel section in the newspaper. Look at the advertising to get a feel for what's being offered to travelers. A lot of schools now offer courses for the different computer reservations systems that you'll have to know; those might enable you to get a job much more easily. But I wouldn't discourage someone just because he or she didn't have any training. A lot of agencies don't mind taking on newcomers who know just a little bit and molding them into what they want their travel agents to be like.

Joanie Blair, 34,
travel agent, Brennco Travel, Kansas City, Missouri
Years in travel: 13

How did you get started in the travel business?
I had gone to a travel college in Portland, Oregon, where I learned a lot of the basics of how the travel industry works. Then I was hired through the school by Braniff Airlines to work as a reservationist. I made flight arrangements and issued tickets.

When Braniff went out of business, I got a job with an American Express travel agency in Kansas City. It was a very high volume, prestigious agency that had a lot of affluent customers who traveled all over the world. Initially I was a leisure agent and sold a lot of vacation packages and cruises and arranged tours for individuals and groups.

What was the hardest part about being a travel agent in the beginning?
Because the agency was in a very high-visibility location, the number of people who walked in to ask questions and make reservations was almost overwhelming. For me, the hardest part was a lack of training. I did have my airline reservations background, but the travel agency used a totally different computer system. I found that having been a reservationist for an airline was of very little benefit, at least in the beginning.

What I needed to know was how to handle clients and their demands. Looking back on it, it probably was a good way to learn, but it sure wasn't an easy way.

What's your current job like?
I'm a senior travel agent working for a large agency that handles both business and pleasure travel. Like many travel agents, I work part time, three days a week, but often it seems that I pull as heavy a load as a lot of people who work five days a week. I do corporate and leisure travel, which means I do some of everything. I plan business trips, sell vacation packages, book cruises—anything my clients want.

What do you like best about it?

I'm crazed about 99 percent of the time, but I love the camaraderie I have with the people in my office and with my clients. Like a lot of agents with some experience, I've had some of my clients for years. Some I've never even met; we've just talked over the phone. But I feel like I know them; you build a trust by doing the work, and the trust turns into a friendship. The biggest challenge is trying to maintain a high level of business travel and combine it with leisure travel.

Why is that important?

Vacation travel is very time-consuming; it often requires extensive research and communicating with hotels, airlines and other travel suppliers all over the world. Corporate travel is more straightforward—business travelers know what they want—and it usually requires less planning. On the other hand, corporate clients are extremely demanding. They expect things to go smoothly.

Because I have family responsibilities, it would be nice to focus on the corporate side and have a little more time at home. But our company is now leaning toward the leisure side of the business because that's where the growth in the industry is. In any case, I've paid my dues and I make a good salary, so I can't complain.

What's the hardest part of the job?

I have a lot of fun with my job, but it's hard work. Sometimes I don't think people can fathom how time-consuming it can be. My husband is an executive at Hallmark, and I don't think he works harder than I do. I have two telephone lines lit all the time, calls holding and calls waiting to be returned. I never have a relaxed moment or time to take a breather. I probably don't take a lunch break nine-tenths of the time. If I didn't enjoy my clients and their friendship so much, I don't think I could do it.

What kind of person makes the best travel agent?

Anyone can be a travel agent—it's not that hard to learn what to do—but not everyone can be a good one. The people in our office are extremely diverse; some are outgoing and extroverted, and others are very quiet.

The secret of being good is understanding your clients, learning how to relate to each one and knowing what their needs and interests are. Each travel agent may go about it differently, but we accomplish the same thing.

How can you stay ahead once you land the job?
Read any information you can find about travel and try to attend seminars and workshops because that's basically how you'll learn. That's also how you meet and build connections. It's also very important to begin to build a client base by doing such a good job that people keep coming back.

Is there anyone who has watched a trio of flight attendants in their smart, crisp uniforms walk briskly through an airline terminal, laughing and smiling, without thinking, "What a great life they must lead"? There's something about these well-dressed, self-confident women and men that suggests glamour and excitement. They *do* work hard, but they also play hard, flying to places most of us only dream about.

Their long hours are often spent cleaning up after sick babies, calming unreasonable people or serving 200 meals in less than an hour. They may spend holidays in lonely hotel rooms thousands of miles from family, and their social life is often catch-as-catch-can because their work schedule is

19

too confusing for most people to keep up with. And until they've gained a lot of seniority, they can't even choose where "home" is.

Flight attendants make sure that the passengers on a commercial or charter airplane trip are safe and happy. In addition to serving drinks and meals, they keep passengers informed about the progress of the flight and hand out magazines and headphones. They're trained to deal with emergency situations—whether it's assisting a passenger who suddenly becomes ill or giving instructions to passengers during unexpected turbulence.

To be a good flight attendant, you have to love two things: people and travel. Passengers can be cooperative or demanding, polite to a fault or downright rude. Some have never flown before and do not understand your role; seasoned travelers may be so accustomed to seeing you that you become "invisible," at least until they need something.

A curiosity about places you've never visited is also a plus. It will help you get through the times when you are stuck between flights in a city you did not choose.

It helps enormously to be an independent, outgoing type who doesn't need the security of being at home or around people you've known for a long time to be happy. Attendants are assigned to bases, usually in major cities where the airline has extensive service. Employees are required to find their own housing and may be transferred or rotated to different bases.

Those who fly long distances or regularly do international service often do not live at home even between flights. They stay in hotel rooms paid for by the airline. The typical attendant is away from home base for about one-third of his or her working hours. If you're on overnight layover, you usually arrive at a destination late, catch a night's sleep, then report for duty the following day.

Because the job of flight attendant attracts far more applicants than there are jobs available, you will have to be determined and persistent to get hired. You'll have to show that you are personable, know how to make people feel relaxed and have the self-confidence to get others to take orders from you.

What You Need to Know

◆ **Getting into the Field**

- ❑ How people behave and how to deal with different personality types
- ❑ U.S. or world geography
- ❑ A foreign language—helpful if you work for an airline with international routes

Necessary Skills

- ❑ Excellent communications skills (to be able to interact with passengers easily)
- ❑ Ability to come up with creative solutions
- ❑ Self-confidence to speak in an authoritative way
- ❑ First aid techniques (you will receive emergency aid training after being hired)

Do You Have What It Takes?

- ❑ A knack for reassuring and calming people
- ❑ A friendly personality
- ❑ Genuine enjoyment of meeting and talking to new people
- ❑ Patience (passengers can be demanding or rude)
- ❑ Assertiveness (to take control of a group of passengers if necessary)
- ❑ Punctuality (the plane won't wait for you)
- ❑ A good sense of humor
- ❑ Ability to stay calm in stressful situations

Physical and Age Requirements

- ❑ Age 19 or older
- ❑ Weight in proportion to height
- ❑ A well-groomed appearance
- ❑ Excellent physical condition and health
- ❑ A pleasant voice
- ❑ Good eyesight (specific policies vary with airlines, but corrected vision is generally acceptable)
- ❑ Stamina (you'll be on your feet for hours at a time)

Education

A high school education is generally required; some airlines prefer some college experience.

Licenses Required

None. Membership in a union, however, is often required after you are hired. The two major flight attendants' unions are the Association of Flight Attendants and the Transport Workers Union of America.

Job Outlook

Job opportunities: very good
Competition for jobs: keen
The trend in the airline industry is toward larger airplanes, which will require more attendants per flight. Overall growth of travel is also predicted, so job openings will grow. Competition is very strong, however. Increasing numbers of attendants are making a career out of their job instead of doing it only for a few years, so fewer openings occur because of retirement. Also, the excellent benefits offered by most airlines, including free travel, attract large numbers of well-qualified applicants.

The Ground Floor

Entry-level job: flight attendant

Newcomers are considered reserve flight attendants and are on call to fill in at the last minute for more senior attendants who may be ill, on vacation or otherwise unable to work. They do not have regular flight assignments. Reserve status lasts a minimum of six months and may last years, particularly for international divisions of the major airlines.

On-the-Job Responsibilities

❑ Attend the preflight briefing with pilot and crew
❑ Prepare the airplane for flight (organize supplies, equipment, meals)
❑ Do a cabin check (make sure there are sufficient blankets, magazines, supplies)

- ❏ Welcome passengers and assist them in finding seats
- ❏ Make flight announcements; explain safety precautions
- ❏ Keep records of in-flight passenger purchases and meals and liquor served
- ❏ Provide information about arrival and connections
- ❏ Sell duty-free items (international flights)
- ❏ Handle medical emergencies
- ❏ Give instructions to passengers and assist them in exiting the plane in an emergency situation

First flight attendants (also called "lead" attendants) prepare paperwork for each flight, supervise the work of the flight crew and handle passenger problems that cannot be resolved by other attendants.

When You'll Work

The government and airline labor agreements limit the number of hours per month attendants may fly—it's usually 75 to 85. Attendants put in about the same amount of hours per month working on the ground, before and after flights.

Because of flight schedules, attendants often work long hours for several days in a row and then have several days off. Bad weather and peak travel times may result in much longer work hours. During very long flights, attendants may have time off while in the air.

Time Off

It's not uncommon to have 11 to 15 days off each month. It is sometimes also possible to trade flights with colleagues in order to schedule a longer period away from the job.

Because the holidays tend to be peak travel times and senior attendants have first choice of vacation time, beginners usually end up working the major holidays, often far from home.

Perks

- ❏ Generous time off
- ❏ Excellent travel benefits for yourself and your family
- ❏ Health, life insurance and retirement plans

Who's Hiring

❑ Scheduled domestic airlines (regional and national)
❑ Charter airlines
❑ Large corporations with their own aircraft (very few jobs)

Scheduled airlines offer service to many destinations on a regular, published schedule. Charter airlines provide service to one or a few destinations only once a day or less. They often fly groups, and flights on these airlines are often sold through tour companies and travel agencies.

Foreign carriers are usually required to hire personnel from the country where the airline is based.

On-the-Job Hazards

❑ Exposure to illness from working in enclosed spaces
❑ Ear or respiratory problems due to changes in air pressure
❑ Jet lag from constantly crossing time zones
❑ Exposure to high altitude radiation (of most concern to pregnant attendants who are often given the option of not flying)
❑ Slight risk of injury from turbulence
❑ Very slight risk of death or severe injury in the event of a plane crash (you're still safer in the air than in a car, however)

Places You'll Go

Beginners and experienced flight attendants: many opportunities for travel

Most companies have a bidding system based on seniority that determines which routes each attendant will be assigned. Senior attendants have first crack at where they want to travel during their working hours. Schedules and routes are often rotated regularly.

You have the benefit of low-cost travel in your time off—you pay only taxes and service charges. And because of reciprocal agreements among airlines, including foreign carriers, attendants are not limited to flying free on their own company's aircraft. Flight attendants' immediate families and spouses are entitled to the same travel privileges.

For beginning flight attendants, travel is restricted because of their reserve status; they must be on call at their home base in case they're needed to fill in for someone else.

Airplanes range from small ten-passenger commuter planes (the flight attendant may be sitting down because the ceiling is low and passing drinks from a cooler because there's no kitchen) to giant jet aircraft carrying almost 500 passengers.

Surroundings

Generally speaking, the bigger your plane, the easier it is to do your job (passengers are less likely to have to squeeze past you, for one thing). The jumbos may have several aisles running the length of the plane, three classes of passenger service (coach, business and first), and an upper deck (sometimes equipped with sleeping berths). Each section has its own kitchen and service station where meal and beverage carts are prepared. Flight attendants generally do not have their own quarters or private work areas, although service stations can be curtained off.

Starting salaries: $13,000-$20,000
Five years experience: $20,000-$27,000
Top earners: $35,000

Dollars and Cents

Flight attendants earn overtime pay if flights are delayed and they must work longer than scheduled. Attendants working international flights often receive higher salaries.

Once attendants come off reserve—after six months to four or five years (time on reserve depends on the airline and the routes you fly; international service usually means a longer time on reserve)—their responsibilities and privileges are the same as those of other flight attendants.

Moving Up

To become a lead or first attendant (sometimes called in-flight manager), you will receive additional supervisory training. These few positions are voluntary and usually are awarded on the basis of seniority. Being an in-flight manager usually means a modest increase in salary, although your earnings as a flight attendant are primarily based on how long you've worked for the company.

Flight attendants can move into other areas of flight service or airline operations. Many become training instructors, supervisors, recruiters or ticket agents.

Where the Jobs Are

The major bases for flight attendants are New York, Chicago, Los Angeles, San Francisco, Dallas/Fort Worth, Miami, Atlanta, St. Louis, Minneapolis/St. Paul, Seattle and Charlotte, North Carolina. But you do not need to live in or near these areas to be hired as a flight attendant.

The Male/Female Equation

While numbers vary from airline to airline, there are considerably more men working as flight attendants today than in years past. Still, the majority are women.

Making Your Decision: What to Consider

The Bad News

❑ Long working hours
❑ No control over where you are based
❑ Work schedules that can put a strain on family and social life
❑ Enclosed, limited work-spaces
❑ Menial tasks

The Good News

❑ Excellent travel and other benefits
❑ Good job security
❑ A chance to meet lots of people
❑ Flexibility in scheduling work
❑ Support and friendship of fellow attendants

Training

Training is provided after hiring and, while many travel schools include courses on airline operations and computer systems, the only way to be trained as a flight attendant is to get the job first. Four- to six-week programs are offered at special flight schools. Courses include safety, emergencies, flight regulations, public relations, human relations, meal service, company policy, schedules and first aid. Trainees also take practice flights.

Trudy Bettinazzi, 31,
flight attendant, American Airlines,
Avella, Pennsylvania
Years in travel: two and a half

How did you become a flight attendant?
I'd always wanted to be a flight attendant as far back as I
can remember. I started interviewing when I was 18, but I
never got past the first interview. I tried again every three
years. At times I thought I'd never get hired. Then American Airlines hired me.

What kind of training or background did you have?
I went to a travel school, which didn't help me get a job,
although it did familiarize me with the industry. I worked
in a sheriff's office and in a bank, both of which involved
working with the public—and that's what being a flight
attendant is all about.

Describe your job responsibilities.
We make sure people are safe on the flight and provide the
best possible service we can. We welcome people on board,
make them comfortable, serve meals, answer questions and
try to make the flight something special.

It's different from a lot of jobs because your duties don't change over time. You become more aware of what you're doing, but you continue to do pretty much the same thing. We're divided into domestic and international service, and international takes a little more experience.

You bid for the routes you want, and you can usually work at what you like best for each flight. Some attendants have what we call "premium qualified" positions with added responsibilities—they do extra paperwork and deal with problems other attendants can't handle. Those jobs require more training.

What do you like best about the job?
I like the flexibility. You can generally work as much or as little as you want. We work about 15 or 16 days a month, and then we're off the rest. But when we work, it's three days or maybe even a week at a time.

And I love meeting people from all different walks of life. The most important attribute a flight attendant needs is compassion. Because if you have first-time travelers, you have to make it special for them. At the same time you have to cater to the business traveler. This could be his or her twentieth trip that month, and you still have to make it special.

The travel benefits are great. As a flight attendant, you can fly anywhere you want in the world, and you can take members of your immediate family with you. My favorite place to go when I have time off is Hawaii.

Was it difficult starting out?
Training was very, very difficult for me. It's only five and a half weeks long, but it's the most intense training I've ever had! And there's no way you can prepare for it—that's what's stressful about it.

When you graduate, they send you immediately from school to your new home base. There's no time to go home, no time to do anything: You graduate at 11 A.M., and you're at your base that afternoon. You have to find an apartment, get settled and go to work a couple of days later. You start out as a reserve attendant, which means you're on call to fill in at any time. So in the beginning, your whole life is lived by your beeper.

Are there any other challenges to the job?

As with any job, some days are better than others. The hardest thing is making people understand that when you're 37,000 feet in the air, there's only so much you can do to make them happy. If you take off without enough meals, you can't go back and get more.

What makes you a good flight attendant?

I think my strongest quality is being a people person. I have a knack for calming people down if something's worrying them: for example, if this is their once-in-a-lifetime vacation and they're going to miss their next flight because we're delayed. That might throw their hotel and car rental reservations.

I think I understand how to deal with experienced travelers, too. To them, every flight is like the one before. So I go out of my way to make it a little different. I have a good memory, so by the time they leave the plane, I know their names.

What advice do you have for someone considering being a flight attendant?

Having a genuine love of people is essential. You have to be persistent and able to take rejection because you might not get hired right away. You also have to be willing to sacrifice. Your first year on the job basically belongs to the airline, and you have to make the decision that your career is the most important thing.

When you're on reserve you have to be at your base because when they beep you, you have to go to the airport. You can find yourself in a strange city during the holidays. It can be rough. Of course, the benefits can make up for a lot, but when you're starting out you have to be willing to give up many things.

Cyndie Anderson, 34,
flight attendant, USAir,
Winston-Salem, North Carolina
Years in travel: seven

How did you become a flight attendant?
I have two sisters who were flight attendants, and I'd always wanted to be one, too. I started out working in the
office of Piedmont Airlines as a secretary. I got married
the same year, and my husband really didn't want me to be
an attendant and be gone from home all the time. I worked
in the office for five years. Then USAir bought Piedmont,
and I wasn't really sure whether I'd have my office job any
longer. I thought it would be easier to keep my job or find
a job with another airline if I were an attendant. So I put in
my request, and it came through.

**Did you have any training in the travel industry before
you got your first job?**
No. I had worked as a secretary, so I had some training in
dealing with people. But I didn't have any travel background.

What was flight attendant training like?
Total stress! Training is really tough; it's mostly safety-
related and prepares you for emergencies. I trained first
with Piedmont's facility. Then, four years ago, when we
all became USAir attendants, we had to get additional training to qualify on the specific types of aircraft that were in
the USAir fleet.

**Did you have to relocate when you became a flight at-
tendant?**
I was lucky starting out because I was based in Greensboro,
which is nearby, so I really didn't have to leave home. My
situation—being hired and able to work from my home-
town—would be unusual now. The airlines have cut back
and closed a lot of bases or hubs.

How would you describe your work?
We take care of the passengers, but our primary purpose is
to make sure everyone is safe and to handle emergencies
when they come up.

The thing about being a flight attendant is that your duties don't really change. You may work different types of airplanes, but you basically do that same job. Sometimes the service is more detailed or extensive. When you're doing transcontinental service, for example, you have more meals to serve and duties to perform.

What was the hardest part about starting out as a flight attendant?
I guess the nervousness. You're unsure about what to do; you think, "Oh gosh, if something happens am I going to panic?" And being away from home can be difficult. We're pretty lucky compared to the routes attendants on some airlines have to fly. The longest time away from home we have is four days, and the least we have is a one-day schedule—out and back in one evening.

I have a two-year-old daughter, and it's still hard to leave her. But then I only work 15 days a month, so I actually have more time with her than if I had a nine-to-five job.

What do you like best about the job?
I don't think there's really anything I *don't* like about it. I love working with so many different people. We have 3,000 flight attendants working out of this area. I love to go to all the different places we fly. I did my first international trip last spring to Frankfurt, which was exciting.

Have you taken advantage of being able to travel?
Oh yes. Because I work for the airline, my family and I can travel anywhere USAir flies, and we get discounts on other airlines as well. So we've been to Hawaii, the Virgin Islands and the Bahamas.

What advice or suggestions would you give someone thinking about a career as a flight attendant?
If you want to have fun and have a great job, then this is it. If you like to travel, then this is the job to do it in. I wouldn't recommend any specific kind of study or travel training school because every airline has its own training. Until you actually are hired and they tell you what you have to learn, there's really nothing you can prepare for. Learning about the rest of the industry would be helpful, but you wouldn't learn much about what a flight attendant does.

Brad Laird, 28,
flight attendant, Tower Air,
Philadelphia, Pennsylvania
Years in travel: five

How did you become a flight attendant?
Strictly by chance. I was working part time at UPS and
also as a catering manager. A friend got a letter for an open
call interview at Eastern Airlines. I ended up going to the
interview and was offered a job at Eastern. But then someone who worked for Tower Air suggested I try them. I did,
and I got hired. I took it strictly because it was more money
than I was making. But now that I'm in it, I love it!

Did you have any background in travel?
None whatsoever. I had a year of college and a year of trade
school studying building renovation.

What do you like about your job?
Nothing is routine. My schedule, my destinations and the
people I work with are always changing. Sometimes I go to
a different climate. Tonight I'm going to Paris, where it's
cold this time of year; next week it might be Miami. And
there's a different group of attendants working each flight,
so there's no routine. I look at each trip as a challenge because I know nothing's going to be ordinary about it.

And I like the independence. There aren't supervisors
breathing down my neck all the time. With Tower Air, it's
like going on a minivacation every week or so.

What kind of training did you get?
We had two weeks of training, basically Federal Aviation
Administration regulations and safety regulations. In-flight
service training lasted two or three hours, and we also
learned company policies and personal grooming.

How long were you on reserve status?
For the first four and a half years I was on reserve schedule,
which meant that I had to be available to be called on a
beeper for five days in a row from either midnight to noon
or noon to midnight. Then I'd have two days off—they're
called X days. But sometimes they would call on the fourth

day of my reserve period and I would fly for a week, so naturally I'd miss out on my X days. When you're on reserve you don't get to pick routes, so you might fly anywhere. And we fly military charter flights all over the world.

What is the work like?
The duties on board the aircraft are pretty much the same on every flight. When we first board, we check emergency equipment. Then we go through the plane and do a security check. When the passengers come on, we help them with seating and luggage, secure the doors and luggage racks, and make sure all belongings are under the seats and that scat belts are fastened. Then we do a safety demonstration, pointing out the exits and how to use emergency equipment. Once we take off, we each have assigned duties, which we do with minimal supervision.

So what is your schedule like?
Well, for example, when I fly to Paris tonight, we'll have 22 hours there before flying to Frankfurt. There we'll have 75 hours, and then we'll come back home. Two days later, I leave for Paris again and stay there a whole week before coming back. My time there is my own. When I go to Paris for a week, I have a nine- or ten-hour work day and then I sit and play in the city for a week because it's a charter flight. Then we fly back home, and that's another working day. So out of a whole week I may have worked just two days.

What don't you like about the job?
You really can't plan for any personal engagements or appointments. Lots of times if you want to go to a doctor or buy tickets for a concert a month in advance, you end up canceling because you get called.

What advice do you have for someone considering a career as a flight attendant?
Have financial and personal flexibility. When you start, your guaranteed salary can be quite low. And for someone who is married or who has kids, I would recommend looking for something else. You have so little control over your schedule, particularly when you're on reserve.

RESERVATIONS AGENT

"Do you offer service between JFK and Miami airports?" "What's the best weekly rate you have on a car in Denver?" "Can you give me more information about your cruises to the Caribbean?" These are the kinds of questions reservations agents get by the hundreds every day. The agents' answers—and the friendliness and skill with which they are provided—often result in customers booking travel or transportation plans with them.

Without reservations agents, no one would fly, sail, drive or take a train anywhere. They're the people who sell the tickets for airlines, cruise lines, tour companies, railway and bus companies, car rental companies and tour operators.

Many reservations agents never work face-to-face with the public. Most work at a kind of reservations central, alongside co-workers who usually wear headsets and sit in front of computer monitors.

Each airline and car rental company has its own automated reservations systems. Many cruise lines and tour operators now use computer systems as well. Reservations agents are among the best trained of all travel industry employees because their success depends on (1) thoroughly understanding the product they are selling, and (2) operating a sophisticated, automated reservations system.

Reservations agents spend their day on the phone, often handling several hundred calls in an eight- or eight-and-a-half-hour period. They give callers information about schedules, fares and routes and book reservations using sophisticated computer systems.

The job requires the self-discipline to sit at a desk all day and do the same task repeatedly without losing your enthusiasm. There is pressure to handle each call quickly and go on the next. A knack for selling is required; you must try to persuade the caller to make a reservation with you instead of calling another company. Some companies even have sales quotas or targets to encourage reservations agents to try their hardest to make the sale. Reservations agents also must have the patience and self-control to project a cheerful, helpful attitude even when dealing with difficult, unreasonable callers.

There are, however, rewards for putting in such a hard day's work. The biggest benefit is travel-related: The company you work for may offer you discounted or free transportation or vacation packages. That's an especially big draw for would-be airlines reservations agents. Cruise lines and tour operators may also offer glamorous discounts.

Working in reservations is a good starting point if you hope to move up within a particular area in the travel industry. In the airline industry, for example, it's the training ground for people who go on to jobs in operations, sales and marketing.

If you're someone who enjoys answering people's questions, likes a fast-paced day and has a great telephone voice and an ability to sell, being a reservations agent may be your ticket to a happy career in travel.

What You Need to Know

❏ Airline and other computer reservations systems— helpful but not essential

❏ Local, national and sometimes world geography

❏ Details about the industry in which you hope to work—air, rail, bus, cruise, tour or car rental

❏ English grammar (so you sound competent and intelligent on the telephone)

❏ A foreign language—useful but not necessary

Necessary Skills

❏ Basic sales techniques (to be able to persuade a caller to buy your product)

❏ Good listening skills (to be able to answer questions and take down reservation information accurately)

❏ Strong communications skills (so you can give information quickly and precisely)

❏ Ability to keep good records

❏ A friendly, courteous telephone manner

❏ Organizational skills to maximize efficiency (you'll be handling 200 phone calls a day)

Do You Have What It Takes?

❏ Self-assertiveness to close a reservations "sale" and meet targets

❏ Self-motivation (to work without supervision)

❏ Ability to handle difficult customers

❏ Self-confidence to come across as authoritative

❏ Ability to handle a large volume of calls daily

❏ Endurance (after eight hours on the phone, you have to still sound eager to please)

❏ Patience in dealing with demanding customers

❏ Ability to do repetitive work

Physical Requirements

❑ A pleasant-sounding and strong voice
❑ No history of lower-back problems (you'll be sitting all day)

Education

No specific courses or degrees beyond a high school education are required.

Licenses Required

None

Job Outlook

Job opportunities: will grow faster than average
Competition for jobs: keen
The travel industry continues to be one of the fastest-growing industries in the world, but there is considerable competition for jobs because of low turnover and a large supply of workers. The airlines in particular attract a large number of qualified people because of their travel benefits.

The Ground Floor

Entry-level job: Receptionist, travel clerk, reservations agent, transportation ticket agent
Many get their foot in the door by working part time, filling in during peak travel periods and holidays.

On-the-Job Responsibilities

Beginners

❑ Answer incoming telephone calls
❑ Provide information about schedules, travel routes and fares (often by accessing computerized reservations data bases)
❑ Assist customers in making travel decisions
❑ Make reservations for domestic and international travel
❑ Close sales by accepting payment in the form of credit cards

❏ Change and cancel reservations
❏ Refer to travel manuals, tariffs and other reference materials

Experienced Reservation Agents

All of the above, plus:
❏ Work with travel agents and other travel professionals to arrange travel for leisure and business clients
❏ Train new employees
❏ Supervise other reservations agents

When You'll Work

Reservations agents generally work five days a week, eight or eight and a half hours a day, often in shifts. Large companies, especially those dealing in international travel, may keep their phone lines open 24 hours a day. Beginners often work the least desirable times—nights and weekends. Expect overtime during peak travel periods such as major holidays and the summer months or when your company offers special discounted fares to leisure travelers. Part-time reservations agents (who are just starting out) may have to work irregular and unpredictable hours.

Time Off

Company policies vary, but you can expect the traditional one- to four-week vacation each year (depending on seniority and company) plus major holidays.

Perks

❏ Free or discounted travel, depending on the type of company (in particular airlines, cruise lines and tour operators)
❏ Familiarization (fam) trips (offered by airlines, cruise lines, tour operators and other vacation companies that want their employees to understand the product they are selling)
❏ Health insurance and retirement plans

Who's Hiring

- Domestic airlines
- Foreign airlines with regularly scheduled flights between the U.S. and other countries
- Cruise lines
- Rail companies
- Tour companies
- Car rental companies
- Bus transportation companies
- Sightseeing companies
- Ferry services

On-the-Job Hazards

- Fatigue from repetitious work
- Eyestrain and headaches from staring at a computer screen
- Lower back pain from sitting all day
- Stress from dealing with difficult customers
- Carpal tunnel syndrome (a wrist injury that can occur from using a computer keyboard for hours every day)
- Hoarseness and other voice problems

Places You'll Go

Beginners: limited to good opportunities
Experienced agents: excellent travel opportunities
Seniority often determines who can travel where and when. This means that beginners often have to settle for leftovers. Nevertheless, travel benefits are probably the single most popular reason for being in the industry.

Employees of many airlines, especially the major carriers and most of the foreign carriers, are allowed free travel on a space-available basis and pay only taxes and service charges. Because of reciprocal agreements among the airlines, you may travel on most other carriers as well. Most airlines also allow immediate family members of employees the same privileges.

Cruise lines generally offer free or reduced-rate cruises to their employees. Carnival Cruise Lines, for example, provides two complimentary cruises a year. Other types of travel companies have their own policies. For example,

Club Med, the all-inclusive vacation packager, provides three vacations a year to its employees at reduced rates.

Travel companies, particularly airlines, cruise lines and tour operators, often offer familiarization (fam) trips to their reservations staff to help them become familiar with the company's product. It is usually not necessary to use vacation time to take a fam trip. And many of the international companies, particularly foreign airlines, sometimes schedule training sessions for reservations agents in home-base cities such as London or Paris.

Employees of bus, car rental, rail and ferry services have fewer travel benefits, although they generally receive discounted travel with their own company.

Most reservations departments, particularly those of large companies, are in downtown office blocks, often in major cities. Increasingly these metropolitan reservations offices are moving to the outskirts of cities as travel companies try to economize with less expensive rents.

The typical reservations office environment is busy, sometimes loud and chaotic, and there is little privacy. Your work space is apt to be a small alcove at best. Reservations agents spend all their workday on the telephone and rarely have face-to-face contact with customers.

◆ **Surroundings**

Starting salaries: $12,000-$18,000
Five years experience: $20,000-$30,000
Top earners: $40,000

◆ **Dollars and Cents**

Airlines have traditionally paid the best, and many still do. But new labor agreements and the generally dismal state of the airline industry's finances have resulted in much lower salaries at many companies. Foreign airlines often pay reservations staff the best starting salaries.

Salaries in other segments of the travel industry vary considerably. As a general rule, larger companies pay better, but there are some very small organizations, especially those offering upscale, expensive products, that offer among the highest salaries in the industry.

Moving Up

Because all travel reservations agents, regardless of experience, do primarily the same job, there is little moving from one job description to another within the reservations department. Instead, many employees move to other departments, including sales and marketing, customer service, finance, computer operations and company operations.

In larger companies it is possible to become a senior reservations agent, supervisor or even city or regional reservations manager. Managerial roles such as supervisor or city reservations manager often include training new reservations staff. In the airlines, reservations agents with a strong sales track record who have the potential to be good "front" people are promoted to ticket agent. They deal one-on-one with the public at walk-in ticket office locations.

Where the Jobs Are

Travel companies and transportation providers are located throughout the United States. The airlines are often based in major metropolitan areas such as New York, Chicago, Dallas, St. Louis and Atlanta, but they often have large reservations centers in smaller cities or even relatively rural areas. Many of the cruise lines are based in Florida or New York. Tour companies can be found on the West Coast and in the Midwest, New York and New England. Car rental companies are scattered all over the country, and Amtrak is based in Washington, D.C., with reservations centers in Chicago, California and Pennsylvania.

The Male/Female Equation

Both men and women work as reservations agents, although a slightly higher percentage are women. The ratio of men to women varies significantly with each company.

The Bad News

- ❏ Repetitious work
- ❏ Stress of handling a high volume of calls or making sales targets
- ❏ Dealing with difficult customers
- ❏ A confining work environment (for some)

The Good News

- ❏ Discounted and free travel (for some)
- ❏ Job security
- ❏ Satisfaction of helping customers make travel decisions and plans
- ❏ A stepping stone to more challenging jobs in the travel industry

◆ **Making Your Decision: What to Consider**

Most companies provide on-the-job training for new employees. Initial training consists of learning the automated reservations system (SABRE, System One, Data II, Covia and Worldspan/PARS are the five major systems), schedules, fares, itineraries, company policies and sales procedures.

You can, however, take travel-related courses at many travel schools and at community colleges. Doing so may give you an advantage in the hiring process because it shows that you are really interested in the industry. But you will still be required to go through the training program of the company that hires you.

◆ **Training**

WHAT IT'S REALLY LIKE

Robert Watson, 25,
senior reservations agent, Cunard Line,
Forest Hills, New York
Years in travel: five

How did you get into the travel business?
I was working in a retail store and mentioned to a customer
that I'd like a change of pace. She made a phone call to
someone she knew at a wholesale travel company that sold
vacation packages to Las Vegas, California and Hawaii. I
got the job, but the company didn't really take off, so I
wasn't there long.

**What was the hardest part about breaking into a job as
a reservations agent?**
The toughest part was having no training. On my second
day, they gave me a brochure, and on the third day they
said, "Here's your phone. Start selling." So I learned how
to talk to the clients and travel agents by myself. But I was
able to use that experience as a way to land a job in reservations with Cunard (the cruise line). They gave me three
weeks of training.

What kind of training was it?

We were taught how to use the computer system, which is specially designed for Cunard. We also learned everything there was to know about our product—the different cabin types in our fleet of what was then seven cruise ships, the facilities on board each ship, the activities, the menus, where each ship went. Customers always ask questions about these subjects, and we must know the answers to get the bookings.

What do you do in your current job?

I handle as many as 200 telephone calls a day. I answer questions and book passengers on the ships. As a senior member of the department, I also do some backup supervisory work and handle some of the difficult customers. About three weeks before each sailing of our transatlantic crossings on the QE2, our largest ship, I'll call people on our standby list and let them know if there's space available and rush to collect payment and send their tickets to them in time.

What kind of travel benefits do you get?

We are offered reduced rate travel on our ships and at our hotels. I've been to London 23 times. One drawback is that we're offered travel on a space-available basis, and the ones I'd like to do most—the Alaska itinerary, the Northern European cruise to places like Denmark and Iceland—are the more popular ones, and they're hard to get on. We have to bid on a seniority basis.

What do you like most about your job?

Talking to people. You get a lot of seniors and retirees who say, "I worked for 30 years, and I told my wife that when I retired we were going to take this vacation as a gift." Or they're going to have a fiftieth wedding anniversary on the QE2. You try to get a cake for them at their table to mark their special occasion.

What's the toughest part of the job?

Fatigue. Handling 200 phone calls a day is repetitive work. You spend a lot of time sitting in front of the computer. And dealing with customers can be trying. I'll get phone calls from people who know very little about travel and what they need to do before they set sail. Three days before they're sailing, they'll say no one told them they needed a passport to go to Russia. And sometimes people don't understand that in this industry there are a lot of things that are out of our control, like weather, for example. Flights get canceled because of a snowstorm, and the passenger can't get to the Caribbean to meet the ship, so he calls us from the airport wanting to know what we can do. Sometimes we can't do anything.

Do you continue getting training once you're on the job?

We've added five ships to the fleet since I started working here, and we go through several days of training to learn the new itineraries, the dining information, any differences in what the new ships offer, how the transportation to the ships works or how the booking procedures differ from what we're used to. If you don't keep on top of what you're selling, you'll have trouble getting ahead.

What advice do you have for someone considering becoming a reservations agent?

Understand that the job itself can be routine, but the benefits make it all worthwhile—so you have to love to travel. How many other jobs allow you to take a cruise vacation for free that normally costs $12,000? You can even get cruise discounts for family members.

Try to take courses to learn computer reservations systems before you apply. Travel experience or a knowledge of geography is helpful, too. Get ahold of travel brochures; get a feel for what different travel companies offer and where they go. Do some research on the products a prospective employer has before you go to an interview so you can ask good questions.

Claudette Pagano, 22,
telephone sales coordinator, British Airways, Jackson Heights, New York
Years in travel: five

How did you get started in the airline business?

Right out of high school, I took a two-month travel course

offered by a local travel agent. I could have worked for the agency as an outside sales agent. But I knew someone who was working for British Air, and I wanted to apply. I interviewed on a Friday and started work the next Monday. It was a matter of being in the right place at the right time.

What was your first job?
I started as a receptionist and worked part time. I met and greeted everyone who came into the building. After about a year, people in the company encouraged me to go into telephone sales, which is reservations. It's excellent experience if you want a future with an airline. It's where everything happens.

Describe your job.
All 300 of us who are in telephone sales are on the phone eight hours a day. We have sales targets to meet as well as incentives for getting additional reservations. We take about 60 to 80 calls a day and try to persuade people to book their flight with British Airways.

Was it difficult in the beginning?
It would have been without the six weeks of training we received. They taught us how to work on the phones, what to say, and all the procedures we're supposed to follow. I also learned the British Airways computer system—I'd never worked on a computer before.

What did you like about doing reservations?
The challenge of persuading a passenger to fly on British Airways. We were given incentives so that if we secured a certain number of credit card bookings, for example, we'd earn a prize. That made it a bit more exciting.

Are there drawbacks to the job?
It can be monotonous at times. And you can get burned out occasionally from dealing with too many difficult customers. But it's just a matter of keeping things in the right perspective. My company prides itself on promoting from within, so there's a definite sense of opportunity.

Have your responsibilities changed since you started?
Absolutely. Now I'm working with three managers and 20 team supervisors to coordinate the whole telephone sales department of 300 people. I assist in organizing and pre-

senting sales incentives. In addition to my job, I am a member of the promotional team for British Airways. We are described as the airline's diplomats and are often the public face of British Airways. Joining the team was quite an achievement.

What kind of travel benefits do you get?
We have incredible travel benefits, not only on British Airways but on U.S. airlines that have exchange agreements with us for services and travel privileges. All we pay are the taxes and service charges, and we can take up to three members of our family or, if we're married, our spouse and children. I've been to Hong Kong shopping, and I was just in France skiing in the Alps for the weekend! We also get training courses in London because that's company headquarters, so I've spent a lot of time there.

In addition to travel, I have three weeks annual vacation, plus a personal day off. We work eight-and-a-half-hour shifts. We bid on shift preferences—there are shifts from 8 A.M. to midnight, but you can also trade with other reservationists. Some people have been able to manage a month or even the summer off and go to Europe by trading schedules with others.

What advice do you have for someone looking for a job with the airlines?
Prepare yourself for interviews by investigating the carrier you are considering. Telephone sales or reservations is a great place to start because there are no limitations on where you can go from there. If you have the ambition and want to move around, there are several other departments you can move into, including finance, computer operations, airport work and legal and public affairs.

Whatever your background or training, if this is what you want, it's just like anything in life—you've got to go for it.

Dawn Davis, 28,
reservations agent, Special Expeditions,
Jersey City, New Jersey
Years in travel: three

How did you get into the travel business?

I was a receptionist at a publishing company and was looking for another job. An employment agency had a receptionist opening at Special Expeditions, which I applied for and got. I answered the phone and directed calls to reservations and other departments, but I also sent out brochures and other materials to people who called. Special Expeditions offers expeditions and voyages to very unusual and remote parts of the world like the Galapagos Islands and the Arctic Circle and also offers educational tours to Europe and other places.

Did you have any training that prepared you?

None. I went to college for two and a half years and majored in accounting.

How did you get promoted?

When I had free time on the reception board, I read all the brochures I could get my hands on so I could learn everything about the company's programs. I let people I worked with know that I'd do anything else that needed to be done. After eight months I was promoted to the operations department, where I was trained to become a program manager. After another year I was promoted to the reservations department.

By the time I moved into reservations, I felt pretty comfortable about our product and I had already been on one of our trips.

What do you do as a reservationist?

We answer all questions about the company and its programs and take reservations. We get probably 80 percent of the calls that come through the switchboard and use a computerized program to make the bookings. We also take brochure requests. People may have questions about the tours or voyages in general or specific questions about a particular problem.

What do you like best about the job?
I really enjoy talking to people, especially when I feel comfortable with the subject I'm talking about. And I like getting in and out of a transaction. I usually talk to a person for ten minutes, then I go on to the next. In some other departments you often deal with the same people and problems over and over again; in reservations you talk to many, many people and you get a feeling of accomplishment.

And I love the travel benefits! Working here I'm able to go on trips and see places I'd probably never see otherwise. I've only been here for three years, and I've already been on two trips. I took a 17-day trip to Europe last year—my first. And I've been on a trip to the Sea of Cortez off the coast of Mexico and Baja California to watch seals and whales. I also go on familiarization trips so when I come back, I can sell those trips that much better. And when we take trips on our vacation time, we can take family members at a reduced rate. We're also paid very well and get health and dental benefits and three weeks vacation.

Did Special Expeditions give you any specialized training?
Basically you just do whatever is necessary for you to be able to answer the questions when handling calls. That's why I set up a binder for myself when I was still a receptionist. But we do get computer training.

What are the challenges of being a reservations agent?
Many of our passengers are older, and sometimes it's difficult to get through to them what they need to know to book the trip. It feels great when you are able to persuade them to take the trip. My great accomplishment happened just the other day when I booked a woman who is taking 13 relatives on one trip. That was very satisfying!

Do you think there's a particular personality that does best in reservations?
You have to be a team player because it's all about getting the job done. You also have to have a lot of patience and endurance. You have to be cheerful even when you might not feel like it because that comes across to the person you're talking to. You can't let them know you might be having a bad day.

What advice do you have for someone who wants to get into reservations?

Read as much as you can, especially about geography. You may have to send someone someplace off the beaten track, and you need to know where it is. I'd also recommend some type of computer training as background, so when you're sitting in front of a computer screen you have an idea of what's going on.

CUSTOMER SERVICE AGENT

"Our luggage didn't make it—and we're going to an afternoon wedding!" "Which gate is flight 211 leaving from?" "Is there any way you can get me on this train?" Customer service agents hear questions and complaints like these every day. They are the problem solvers on the front line for their companies. How well they do their job can make the difference between a dissatisfied customer and one who does repeat business.

Customer service agents are the airline personnel who sell you a ticket, check you and your baggage in or direct you to your flight. They're the people behind the counter when you go to rent a car. They're the men and women who answer questions or sell tickets at train stations and bus depots.

They're the people you go to when your suitcase has disappeared somewhere between Denver and Dallas. In short, they are their company's human face: It is the customer service agent who gives American Airlines, Alamo Rent-A-Car or Amtrak a personality.

Although customer service agents perform a wide variety of jobs, they all spend their working hours dealing with the public face-to-face, often in terminals but sometimes in downtown offices or in locations near airports. Whether their job title is baggage service manager, gate agent or car rental representative, they answer hundreds of questions and resolve dozens of customers' crises, big and small, every day.

The best customer service agents are people who are challenged by problems that must be solved quickly. They don't mind working in the midst of confusion and may even thrive on it. They can calmly address a frantic business traveler whose suitcase was never put on the flight or a family with small children that has missed an important connection.

Keeping *your* self-control when people who want something from you have lost *theirs* is one of the biggest challenges for customer service agents. Remember the scene from *Home Alone* when Kevin's mother loses her temper because the ticket agent cannot get her home on Christmas Eve? Despite her hysteria, the agent keeps his cool.

And it may not be just one or two unhappy people you must placate, but several hundred. When you're the airline gate agent who must tell 300 people they will have to change their plans because the plane is snowbound in Boston, chances are good that you'll have several frustrated individuals to deal with. The customer may not always be right, but it's your job to keep smiling and come up with alternatives, however unreasonable he or she may be.

There will be rewards for your efforts. Many travel companies, particularly the airlines and cruise lines, offer generous travel benefits to their employees.

Your satisfaction will come from knowing that you've made someone's life a little easier. If you like the idea that you can reduce someone's anxiety or even put a smile on the face of a grouch, becoming a customer service agent may be right for you.

What You Need to Know

❏ Familiarity with industry computer systems—helpful but not essential
❏ Local, regional or world geography (depends on the area serviced by your employer)
❏ Basics of group and human psychology
❏ How to speak English well
❏ A foreign language—useful but not necessary

Necessary Skills

❏ Basic math to calculate rates and charges (for those who sell tickets or take on-the-spot reservations)
❏ Excellent listening skills to understand travelers' needs
❏ Excellent communications skills (to give directions or explain how or why something can or cannot be done)
❏ Good organization skills to keep track of details and customers' needs

Do You Have What It Takes?

❏ A calm, reassuring manner
❏ Empathy for people's problems
❏ Ability to deal with all kinds of people politely and fairly
❏ Enthusiasm for solving problems
❏ A friendly personality
❏ Patience (customers can be rude, demanding and downright difficult)
❏ Resourcefulness
❏ Willingness to explain the same information repeatedly without sounding irritable
❏ Self-confidence (to win the trust of your customers)

Getting into the Field

Physical Requirements

❑ A well-groomed appearance
❑ Stamina (you have to be on your feet a lot)

Education

A high school diploma is all that's needed.

Licenses Required

None

Job Outlook

Job opportunities: very good
As long as the travel industry continues to grow, the market for customer service agents will be strong. But there is stiff competition for open positions due to low turnover. (Employees are reluctant to leave because of the benefits, particularly in the airlines and cruise lines.) Also, because of the relatively high number of part-time positions in the field, the number of full-time positions is limited.

The Ground Floor

Entry-level job: ticketing or baggage clerk, cruise line check-in and "welcome aboard" staff, receptionist

On-the-Job Responsibilities

Beginners

❑ Check baggage
❑ Answer questions about departure times and gates
❑ Direct passengers to their flight, train or ship
❑ Staff information desks in airports or transportation terminals
❑ Assist more experienced staff
❑ Check in passengers
❑ Assist in boarding passengers

Experienced Customer Service Agents

- ❑ Process tickets
- ❑ Answer questions about departure times and gates
- ❑ Resolve problems (ticket changes, lost luggage, medical emergencies)
- ❑ Input reservations on computer
- ❑ Sell and exchange tickets
- ❑ Sell travel insurance
- ❑ Assist travelers in making travel plans and decisions (particularly when working in downtown ticket offices where the job combines customer service and reservations)
- ❑ Run credit checks on passengers booking travel
- ❑ Supervise ground services staff at transportation terminals
- ❑ Provide assistance for travel groups and disabled passengers

◆ **When You'll Work**

Customer service agents generally work an eight- or eight-and-a-half-hour day, but often at irregular times. Work hours coincide with the company's schedule of operations, and since most customer service agents work at airports, cruise terminals or bus or train stations, they work when planes, ships and trains arrive and depart.

You can count on overtime at peak travel periods and holidays, and long hours of work during bad weather if your job is at an airport. When flights are delayed, it is customer service agents who handle many of the problems of rebooking missed flights and deal with passenger complaints.

◆ **Time Off**

Customer service agents have the same vacation schedule as other company employees—from one to three or four weeks vacation each year. Time off on major holidays often is given on a seniority basis, so as a beginner, you may find yourself on duty on holidays, although you will be paid overtime.

Perks

❏ Free or discounted travel, depending on the type of company
❏ Familiarization (fam) trips
❏ Health insurance and retirement plans

Who's Hiring

❏ Domestic airlines
❏ International airlines (for jobs in U.S. cities where they have service)
❏ Cruise lines
❏ Car rental companies
❏ Railroads
❏ Vacation companies such as Club Med
❏ Bus companies
❏ Automobile clubs (which use travel advisors who plan travel routes and trips for members)

On-the-Job Hazards

❏ Stress-related problems from dealing with crises
❏ Fatigue from being on your feet all day

Places You'll Go

Beginners: limited to good travel opportunities
Experienced agents: excellent travel opportunities
Employees of many airlines, especially the major carriers, are allowed free travel on a space-available basis. You pay only taxes and service charges, and, because of reciprocal agreements among the airlines, you may travel on most other carriers as well. Most airlines allow immediate family members of employees the same privileges.

Cruise lines generally offer free or reduced rate cruises to their employees. Carnival Cruise Lines, for example, provides two complimentary cruises a year. Other types of travel companies, such as those offering all-inclusive vacation packages, have their own policies. Club Med, for example, provides three vacations a year to its employees at reduced rates.

In addition to free or reduced rate travel that you can use during your vacation time, travel companies such as cruise lines, some airlines and vacation packagers often offer familiarization (fam) trips to their employees to help them get to know the company's product, particularly when a new product or service is introduced. It is usually not necessary to use vacation time to take a fam trip. Those who work for companies based abroad may also be sent to home-base cities for additional training.

Customer service agents generally work at the point of departure and arrival for their company's service. This means you'll be working in airports, cruise ports, transportation terminals, large hotels with airline counters, car rental counters, bus depots and railway stations.

◆ **Surroundings**

The character of these locations varies considerably. Some airports can be large and chaotic; others are small and relatively quiet. Cruise ports vary depending on their location; Miami, which is the cruise capital of the world, has glamorous, palm tree-lined facilities, while New York's relatively new cruise terminal has an unmistakable big-city atmosphere.

While there is usually a staff lounge or even company offices on site, most customer service personnel work in public areas, either behind counters displaying the company name and logo or in the midst of departing and arriving passengers. Car rental customer service agents sometimes work at downtown rental locations in major cities.

Starting salaries: $15,000-$18,000
Five years experience: $20,000-$35,000
Top earners: $45,000

◆ **Dollars and Cents**

Salaries vary considerably depending on the type of company. Airlines usually offer the highest pay scale, in part because airline customer service positions often involve higher levels of responsibility than similar job titles in other segments of the industry.

Within the travel industry, the category of customer service agent includes a number of different jobs: ticket

◆ **Moving Up**

clerks, gate agents, baggage service personnel, ticket agents and "meeters and greeters," among others. Within the airline industry there are even a number of jobs within the framework of customer service, so it is possible to move from one to another and take on additional responsibility. In other travel businesses, such as car rentals, the title customer service agent means just one thing—the person who meets customers at the car rental counter and processes their reservations.

Moving up the ladder of success generally means becoming a supervisor (by demonstrating your ability to train or give directions to others) and possibly a city or regional manager within the customer service department.

Where the Jobs Are

Customer service jobs in the travel industry can be found throughout the United States, wherever large travel companies that have a great deal of interaction with the public are located—usually metropolitan areas large enough to have railway stations, bus depots and airports. Jobs with cruise companies are located in ports—notably Miami and other Florida cities, New York, San Francisco, Los Angeles and ports in Puerto Rico and a few other Caribbean islands.

The Male/Female Equation

Women slightly outnumber men as customer service agents.

The Bad News	*The Good News*	**Making Your Decision: What to Consider**

The Bad News

❑ Stress from constant crises
❑ Little privacy or quiet
❑ Very public work areas
❑ Fatigue from standing on your feet all day
❑ Limited opportunity for advancement

The Good News

❑ Free or low-cost travel
❑ A good level of job security
❑ Opportunities to meet many different people every day
❑ Satisfaction of solving people's problems
❑ Excitement of working at a hub of travel operations

Training

Customer service agents are usually trained by their employer after they're hired. Training may be done on the job, or as is often the case with airlines, at a home base. New employees learn the company's automated reservations system and information on schedules, fares, itineraries, policies and sales procedures. There may also be training in medical emergencies and human relations.

WHAT IT'S REALLY LIKE

Cal Witchard, 38,
customer service agent, America West,
Chicago, Illinois
Years in travel: eight

How did you get into the airline business?
I had been going to college, but I needed work. I walked
into a travel agency because I was curious about their jobs.
They recommended a travel school, so I followed their
advice. When I completed the program, I started as a travel
agency trainee. I subsequently worked for several travel
agencies and then got a job working for a tour operator,
Trade Wind Tours, doing reservations and operations. I got
my current job by following up a help-wanted ad.

What does your job involve?
I work at LaGuardia Airport and primarily sell and exchange airplane tickets. I also check in people and their
luggage, direct them to the gate where their flight is and
answer their questions. I have to be resourceful and have
the answers. I really enjoy what I'm doing.

What do you like most about it?
Two things: the interaction with people and the travel bene-

fits. I really like working with the public, spending the day dealing with a variety of people and their questions or problems. But a major reason to do the job is the travel benefits. We have the same benefits as everyone else in the airline, which means that we get a lot of travel at very little cost. And we're not limited to America West flights. I have three kids, and I have plans to take them to Europe.

What are the challenges of the job?
People who come up at the very last minute to purchase a ticket. Getting everything entered into the computer correctly takes time, and people who are in a hurry don't always understand that.

I'm very friendly, and I don't easily get upset with difficult people; otherwise the job would be really tough. I've been on the other side—I can identify with people when they're under stress or in a hurry and need answers or a ticket so they can get on the plane. I just try to calm them down and try to put myself in their shoes, especially if there's been a flight cancellation or delay. They want to know what's going on; I've found that being apologetic and up-front is the best thing to do.

Does it take a certain kind of personality to be a good customer service agent?
I don't think there is a typical personality. Everyone has his or her own style of working. Some are much friendlier than others; some are very direct, to the point of seeming cold at times. But they get the job done, and that's the most important thing. After all, what people want is help or information. But you do have to like to work with people; you can't do this job day in and day out otherwise.

What do you recommend to someone trying to get a job with the airlines?
Take courses in geography and computers. There are a lot of good community colleges that have courses in airline operations—how to make a reservation and write tickets, how to use the computer. Definitely try to get a lot of experience in computers because you'll be using them all the time, and the more familiar you are with the basics, the better off you'll be starting out. Knowing a second language is a definite plus in getting a job.

Also be persistent, because competition is tough. I once interviewed for a job that 40 others were competing for—something I found out once I was hired. You're probably going to have to start off working part time, which may be a drawback because, at least with this company, you don't get all the benefits, like health insurance, until you're full time. But you can still get travel benefits if you work part time.

Lidinn Perez, 37, baggage service agent, Delta Airlines, Ridgewood, New York
Years in travel: five

Why did you get into the airline business?
I worked for an optician and as a cashier in a bank. Both involved working with the public, and I think that's been the best training for the airline industry. I love to travel, so I figured the airline business would be the one to get into.

My first airline job was with Pan American. I did ticketing and worked as a gate agent and a baggage service agent. I really enjoyed it very much, but when the company went bankrupt, I moved on. I've been with Delta for three years.

What kind of training have you had?
The airlines send you wherever their home base is to study what you've been hired for and to learn the company's policies for operations. I had training with Pan Am and then again with Delta. Delta initially gave me three weeks training as a ticket agent because that's what I started out doing for them at the airport. Whenever you change jobs, you have to go for further training in the new job; for instance, I went for a two-day training program for baggage service.

How would you describe your current job?
I work at LaGuardia Airport. A lot of the job is dealing with problems that started somewhere else. People come into our office when their luggage doesn't make it or has been lost. We try to make sure that all bags that come late are then sent to the right place or the right flight. When a

flight is delayed, we have to send the bags out on the next flight. And we deal with customer complaints all day long. People sometimes come in with the tiniest little thing— their bag is ripped or missing a wheel. So we take down information about their claim and try to help them out.

What's the secret to doing the job well?
Always be pleasant, make sure the passengers are very content, keep a smile on your face and have a good attitude. It's really a matter of learning control; you've got to have it to deal with the public every day, and it's not always easy. A lot of it is understanding people and getting them to understand you. It can take time to locate luggage, and they don't always understand that. Even though I didn't lose their bag, they act as if I did. But the customer is always right.

It sounds stressful. Do you like doing it?
Six months ago I would have said the reason I do this job is for the excellent travel benefits we get. But I've found what I really enjoy about the job is working with the public. I like to help people, to know that I can do something nice for them. When I can send someone home with a big smile, then I feel good. That person's also more likely to fly with us again, and that makes me happy because I know I'll always have a job as long as people keeping coming back to us.

What advice would you give someone who's thinking about an airline job?
Come in with a good attitude. The right attitude toward your job will make all the difference in your success. A good sense of humor, going with the flow and smiling are all important.

Be prepared to work nights, weekends and any other time. And recognize that you may be asked to transfer to other job sites, even other states. Getting in isn't easy, but if you're determined, you can have a very good career.

Mary Kate McCaffrey, 25, customer sales representative, Hertz Rent-A-Car, Cleveland, Ohio Years in travel: eight

How did you get started in the car rental business?
While I was in high school, I worked for a cooperative office education program—we'd go to school in the morning and work in the afternoon. I worked for National Car Rental. I recorded the rental car contracts for the previous day, did filing and answered telephones.

How did you arrive at your present job?
I got laid off from the job with National and got a job with Thrifty Car Rental. With Thrifty, I was renting the cars— handling the customers and arranging for them to rent a car—and also doing licensing of the cars and title work. My next job was with Hertz.

Did you have any training for these jobs?
I had no experience in the travel industry before I started. With Thrifty, it was on-the-job training. They showed me how to make a reservation, told me about the different types of cars they offered, explained their rules about car rentals. I also observed other employees renting cars to customers, and by watching them, and through trial and error, I learned what to do.

Hertz has a two-week training program that they send all new employees to. I went to Philadelphia for two weeks and was in school from nine to five. They taught us the history of the company, everything involved in doing the job and how to use their computers.

What do you do on a day-to-day basis?
I set up reservations that come in the night before, and I make sure I have the cars I need to cover those reservations. I talk to customers on the phone and make reservations for them. When customers come in, I rent them a car or process their returned car. When I started, it was all done by hand, but now we use computers and do it in half the time.

What was the hardest part about starting out?
The hardest part was having customers standing in front of
me and not being sure what I was doing. I worried about
giving them the wrong price for renting the car or whether
they were qualified to rent a car. When I was unsure, I
would ask a more experienced person if I was right. But
I'd do it in such a way that the customer didn't know I was
new.

Tell me about your present job.
I work at Cleveland Hopkins Airport and rent cars, return
cars and make reservations. I work some nightshifts and,
because there's no manager on duty then, I have to help out
if there's an accident or a car breaks down. When I work at
night, I also have to get things prepared for the following
day—if someone wants a specialty car, I have to make sure
the garage men have it ready for the dayshift. And I prepare
reports on the business of the day. During the dayshift, it's
primarily renting and returning cars and answering the telephone.

Do you like working at an airport?
I prefer it—it's busy most of the time. You not only help
customers but everyone else, because you're very visible
and out in the midst of everything going on. So you help
people find their flight, or you tell people where to find a
taxi or bus service. Most car rental companies have airport
counters, but some, like Thrifty, have an off-airport location, which means they're near, but not in, the airport.

What do you like best about your job?
I like helping people out and making things easy for them.
And, I'm really interested in cars, so I'm able to answer
questions and help customers choose what they want or
need. It's not critical to be into cars, though; if you know
the sizes of the cars you can do the job.

**Is there one part of the job that gives you the most satis-
faction?**
Yes. The rental companies have strict regulations as far as
who they'll rent a car to. Generally, you have to show a
valid driver's license and a credit card in your name, and
you have to be over 25. But sometimes we'll have a customer who doesn't fit the regulations. I can decide whether

to bend the rules. You have to make the right decision on the basis of the few minutes you spend speaking with the person, the way they present themselves and your past experience with similar situations. I enjoy being able to make that decision and help someone out.

What don't you like about the job?
The hours. Car rental companies are open every day of the year, 24 hours a day. I work a 40-hour week with some overtime if I'm needed, and I get paid overtime. We have a shift bid every six months when we request certain hours and days to work, and it goes by seniority. Even though I've been here for three years, I'm pretty close to the bottom right now, so I work a dayshift three days a week and a nightshift two days a week. The ideal working hours would be Monday through Friday, 7 A.M. to 3:30 P.M.

The job can also be tiring, depending on the season. During the summer I worked on Saturdays, and it was nonstop wedding parties and vacationers. We were on our feet all day, whereas in the wintertime it slows down and you do get to sit and relax.

What advice would you give someone thinking about working in customer service with a car rental company?
You have to really like to deal with people because that's all you're going to be doing all day long. A little computer experience isn't mandatory, but it would be helpful. Knowing how to type also would help. If you're still in high school, it would be useful to get a job in which you are dealing with the public.

Are there certain personal qualities that are necessary to do your job well?
You need to be able to make quick decisions and think on your feet. And you have to be able to handle difficult customers without taking it personally. You don't know what put them in a bad mood. If they are very upset, you try to do things to soothe them—not just to make things easier on yourself but to make sure customers will come back to Hertz or to whatever company you work with. And you definitely have to be patient and tolerant. A sense of humor always helps, too.

"Look out your window and you'll get a fabulous view of the Golden Gate Bridge. It took four and a half years to build, and it celebrated its fiftieth birthday in 1987." Those might be the words of a tour manager in San Francisco. But no matter where the tour is being given, tour managers can rattle off all kinds of facts and answer almost any question about what tourists are seeing.

Tour managers (often called tour guides or tour directors) are in charge of groups that want to learn everything they can in a certain amount of time, whether it's several hours or several weeks, about a city, state, region, country or several countries. Good tour managers never tire of looking at or talking about their subject, no matter how many times they've done it before.

71

Who is cut out for this kind of work? Those with enormous curiosity who like to research things that interest them and who enjoy sharing what they learn with others. Tour managers are independent types who like to be in control and who get pleasure from playing the role of parent, companion and guide to tourists.

Most tour managers work only six to nine months a year, during which time their living expenses are paid. They may stay in the best hotels and eat in the finest restaurants, or, if it's a budget tour, they may find themselves in less luxurious accommodations.

When tour managers are working, however, there may be little or no time off—tours may run back to back. Finding time for yourself can also be difficult when you're responsible for making sure that everyone's problems are being tended to and confirming the next day's arrangements.

And the travel itself can sometimes be tedious, even though you may be in as grand a place as Yosemite National Park or the French Quarter of New Orleans. That's because getting there may involve eight hours of bus travel—one of the most common ways people tour the United States.

It's not easy to break into the world of escorted tours, particularly if you want to work for a major tour company. Maturity, a knack for leading groups of people, a passion for travel, the ability to learn quickly and a high energy level are important. Many applicants have worked in other areas of the travel industry, especially in front-line jobs in which they have learned to deal with the public on a daily basis. Some tour managers have backgrounds in such people-oriented fields as nursing and teaching.

One of the best ways to get experience is to lead tours locally, part time, perhaps even on a volunteer basis at first. Most metropolitan areas and even smaller communities with historic places or unique attractions offer bus tours, walking tours or tours of local attractions. You'll build up confidence, develop your public speaking and research skills and find out the most effective ways to deal with individuals and groups of tourists. With a little luck, you'll be on your way to a fun-filled career as a tour manager.

What You Need to Know

- ❏ Local, U.S. or world geography (depending on the type of tour you lead)
- ❏ U.S. and world history
- ❏ How to recognize regional birds, animals and plants
- ❏ A foreign language—if you're working in another country or with foreign tourists

Necessary Skills

- ❏ Good public speaking skills
- ❏ Resourcefulness (to deal with requests and crises)
- ❏ Ability to stay organized (to make the tour run smoothly)
- ❏ Ability to lead and control groups of people
- ❏ Research skills (to look things up in the library and assemble information into tour scripts)
- ❏ First aid techniques—helpful but not essential

Do You Have What It Takes?

- ❏ Sensitivity to people's comfort level
- ❏ Ability to think quickly
- ❏ A take-charge personality and a strong sense of responsibility for others' welfare
- ❏ Ability to work with no supervision
- ❏ A knack for warming up to people quickly
- ❏ Ability to entertain and even perform
- ❏ Common sense
- ❏ A sense of humor
- ❏ Patience (your charges can be demanding)

Physical Requirements

- ❏ Great stamina (days can be long and tiring)
- ❏ A well-groomed appearance
- ❏ An iron stomach (to be able to eat anything, anytime)
- ❏ No lower back problems (you will spend hours sitting in buses, trains and other vehicles)

Education

There are no specific educational requirements, but a strong knowledge of geography is important. Foreign language fluency is essential for international guides and for working with foreign groups coming to the U.S. About 60 percent of all tour guides do not have a four-year college education.

Licenses Required

Generally, none, except in New York, New Orleans, Washington, D.C., and Montreal, where guides giving commentary about city sights are required to have licenses. To get one, you must pass a written test, which covers facts about the basic sights of the city.

Job Outlook

Job opportunities: good
Competition for jobs: keen

The tour industry is expanding partly because of government deregulation of the bus industry, which has opened the business to greater numbers of companies. There are roughly 600 tour companies that hire tour managers in the U.S. Many industry experts predict a large increase in escorted tours in the future. But the competition for tour manager jobs is fierce, and the qualifications for getting hired are increasing.

The Ground Floor

Entry-level job: tour manager, tour guide, tour leader or director

On-the-Job Responsibilities

Beginners

❑ Conduct tours of attractions and provide commentary on their history, culture and purpose
❑ Supervise the tour group to make sure members stay together, get back on the bus and stay out of harm's way (in some cities, the tour guide drives the bus as well)

❑ Meet groups at airports, transfer them to hotels and assist with luggage and check-in
❑ Collect payment for the tour

Experienced Tour Guides, Managers or Directors

In addition to the above, they may also:
❑ Escort regional, national or international bus tours that range in length from a few days to several weeks
❑ Make sure all hotel and dining arrangements are in order and confirmed
❑ Work with staff of hotels, restaurants and sightseeing attractions to provide facilities and services for the tour group
❑ Deal with medical or other emergencies
❑ Entertain the tour group while traveling with stories, information or games
❑ Sell "optionals" (excursions for entertainment or sightseeing that are not included in the tour price)

When You'll Work

Only in cities where the weather is warm all year or in those that tourists visit regardless of the weather is there year-round work for guides. Tour managers who escort tours in the U.S. work four to eight months a year, often April through October.

Those who escort long-distance groups often work non-stop 250 days a year. Many do back-to-backs, which means taking one tour right after another, often for weeks or even months at a time. Daily hours can be from dawn until the last group member is in bed.

Most tour managers who work 12 months a year are international tour managers or directors who move with the seasons or who work for companies large enough to offer programs in many parts of the country or the world.

Time Off

Tour guides who give local sightseeing tours may work eight-hour days for peak months of the year and sporadically when there are few tourists in their city. Those who lead groups on tours of several days or weeks usually have little time off between tours, but possibly months off between seasons of work.

Perks

❑ Health insurance option for full-time employees
❑ Opportunities to take free or reduced rate tours
❑ Free or reduced rate accommodations or meals (for experienced managers who travel on their own to set up or deal with hotels and restaurants)
❑ Chance to bring a guest or spouse along on a tour you're leading without charge (sometimes)

Who's Hiring

❑ Local sightseeing companies
❑ Regional, national and international tour companies
❑ Inbound tour companies (handling foreign groups coming to this country)
❑ Special interest tour companies (focusing on sports or art, for example)
❑ Cruise lines (for shore excursion staff)
❑ Travel agencies (those that run local tours or have their own tour programs)
❑ Many tour managers also market their guide and convention greeting services to local and regional organizations and corporations.

On-the-Job Hazards

❑ Transportation-related accident risks
❑ Exposure to illness due to close contact with people
❑ Stress-related problems
❑ Lower back strain from sitting in buses

Places You'll Go

Beginners and experienced managers: frequent opportunities for national or international travel

Except for guides who conduct city sightseeing tours, tour managers spend their working hours traveling. Some guides escort local or regional programs, while others may take groups all over Europe, the Far East or South America. People who work with the shore excursion staff on cruise ships may find themselves anywhere in the world, depending on their company.

Whether they are escorting regional or international tours, most guides spend the majority of their working life away from home. Only local sightseeing guides have the opportunity to work close to home.

Tour managers spend their time on buses, in hotels and restaurants and at sightseeing attractions and national parks. Some tours require considerable time outdoors.

Most tour buses come equipped with restrooms and reclining seats, and some even have televisions and VCRs. Nonetheless, the space can be confining during a long day on the road.

◆ Surroundings

Starting salary: $18,000-$25,000
Five years experience: $35,000-$45,000
Top earners: $60,000 plus

How much you make depends on how much you work. Local sightseeing guides receive tips and are usually paid an hourly rate, which ranges from $8 to $12, depending on the company and seniority. Multilingual sightseeing guides usually earn an additional $5 an hour.

Tour managers receive a combination of salary, daily expenses, a small stipend in place of health insurance (not all companies offer this to all guides), commissions for selling optional excursions, and tips (often 30 percent of a guide's total income). The top earners are often those who lead international tours or who can lead tours in several languages.

◆ Dollars and Cents

Some tour managers who enjoy doing their job choose not to move up. But those with that ambition can. Local guides, for example, have the option of moving into tour manager positions.

Tour managers who stay in the business for many years may move from regional to national to international com-

◆ Moving Up

panies. Or they may move into other areas of tour operations. These include marketing and sales, tour planning, operations and negotiating with suppliers—hotels, restaurants and sightseeing attractions—to put tour packages together.

Requirements for international tour managers include expertise in one or more foreign languages, extensive travel experience (preferably in the region of the world the program focuses on) and knowledge about that region's history, cultures and people.

Where the Jobs Are

While many tour companies are based in major cities, most offer programs all over the U.S. and the world. Where you live doesn't matter as much as what you know about different regions or countries because you will be sent to lead tours in areas you are familiar with. In the U.S., tour companies generally focus on New England, California, the Pacific Northwest, the Southwest and Florida, as well as the major cities.

The Male/Female Equation

Both men and women work as tour managers.

Making Your Decision: What to Consider

The Bad News

❑ Very long hours
❑ Stress from dealing with complaints and problems
❑ Having to be on call and "on stage"
❑ Living in hotel rooms for weeks at a time
❑ No predictable salary

The Good News

❑ Living in style and comfort at employers' expense
❑ Traveling to the most beautiful parts of the U.S. and the world
❑ Seasonal work that can mean long periods of time off
❑ Interacting with people from all parts of the world
❑ Setting your own work schedule

◆ **Training**

High schools sometimes offer courses in travel management, and full programs are offered by travel schools and community colleges. Courses cover tour management, group management, psychology, communication skills, emergencies and advice on finding jobs. Most offer experience in escorting a tour. Some schools prefer to take students who already have some work experience dealing with the public or those with travel experience. Two major tour management schools are:

International Tour Management Institute
625 Market Street, Suite 1015
San Francisco, California 94105
415-957-9489

International Guide Academy
Foote Hall, Suite 313
7150 Montview Boulevard
Denver, Colorado 80220
303-794-3048

In addition, many travel agencies and tour companies offer their own training programs to new employees.

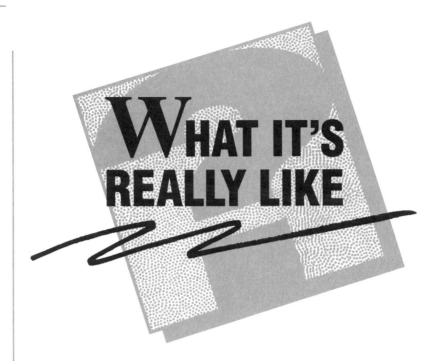

What It's Really Like

Diane Douglas, 43,
freelance tour director,
Salt Lake City, Utah
Years in travel: 15

How did you get started?
My father was a ground instructor and my mom was a pilot
in World War II. And both of my brothers spent years in
the Air Force. After high school I went to work with United
Airlines as a ground services agent. I did that for 13 years.

What do you do now?
I work four months a year as a tour director. I also do some
local guiding, and occasionally I meet groups at the airport
and get them settled in hotels. I sometimes do hosting at
conventions, but during the seven to eight months in the
winter I'm mainly a glass artist. It used to be a hobby, but
after four years I went full time and quit my airline job.
Being a tour director allows me time to create mainly gal-
lery pieces.

Is it typical for tour leaders to have another job?
We're not all artists, but it is very common for tour guides

to do something else when they're not working. Many of us are doing tour guiding as a second career.

How did you get started?
I was referred to the International Tour Management Institute in San Francisco. Even with my airline experience, the major tour companies said, "Go to school or we won't talk to you." I took a two-week course. Because a lot of the job is doing commentary on the bus as you take the group from place to place, the school took us on a three-day field trip and we had to use the microphone and talk about a subject.

What was the hardest part about starting?
The feeling that I'd been thrown into something and I was on my own. Soon after I got out of tour school, I was hired, and I was immediately sent to do a Nova Scotia tour through New England and eastern Canada. I'd never even been there! My company did send me out on my first two-week tour with another woman who had been with the company for years. You have to pick up ideas from other people, see how they handle things and add what you learn to your repertoire.

What would be a typical assignment for you?
My favorite tour starts in Las Vegas. It's a 13-day motorcoach tour that goes to the Grand Canyon, Lake Powell, Bryce Canyon, Zion National Park, Salt Lake City, Jackson Hole, Yellowstone National Park and the Mount Rushmore area. Then I'll meet another group that same day, and the following afternoon we'll leave from Denver and head south through Colorado into northern New Mexico, Santa Fe, Taos, over to Durango, Vail, and Aspen and then back to Denver.

I've got to study every little town that we go through on each trip to know its background and history. You have to know every mountain range and hilltop out both sides of the bus and all the wildflowers and animals. I'm continually on the phone to reconfirm arrangements further down the road.

Do you like the work?
It's a good balance to being alone all winter. Suddenly I'm thrust into a situation where I have a 12- to 14-hour day,

and the only time I look at the clock is to see how far behind I'm running. It's the hardest job I've ever had, but I know I'm going to get all my days off in a row at the end of the season.

It surprised me that I enjoy being with people so much. As a tour director I get a little more time to get to know my passengers. And the contacts last for years.

Another benefit is that I really don't have any expenses for the five months or so of the year that I'm working. So I can concentrate on the art that I want to be doing the rest of the year.

I'm a backpacker and camper kind of a person, so it's a real thrill to me that even though the national parks are crowded, I get to go through them every couple of weeks.

What's the most difficult aspect of the job?
The working conditions can be difficult. During my first summer as a guide, the tour left from New York City. It was a 13-day program, and I was supposed to live in a hotel room in New York from July through October. Luckily I found a friend's apartment—an artist's loft that was heaven—but I had a bellyful of New York and being away from home that long.

And a crowded tour can be difficult. There are days when you hit the bus at 7:30 or 8 A.M. in Rapid City, have a 20-minute rest stop in the morning and an hour for lunch, then hit it to Denver as fast as you can go because you've got people who are going to the airport that afternoon.

It is also difficult to maintain a relationship unless the person you're involved with is in the business with you. But my older brother did this for five years before he opened his own tour company, and he's still married.

What advice would you give someone considering becoming a tour guide?
First, unless you're outgoing and confident, you're going to have a hard time. You've got to be onstage as long as people in the group are around, and you really have to enjoy constant interaction with them. You should love to do research, which I spend more time on than I do leading tours.

Tony Rende, 33,
tour director, AAW Travel,
Brooklyn, New York
Years in travel: 15

How did you get started in the travel business?
My cousin started a tour company and asked me if I could
conduct some tours. I was 18 and just out of high school.

What was your first job?
We called it trip directing. I went to hotels in the Catskills
and the Poconos and greeted groups on arrival, made sure
everything was set for them and that their week went
smoothly, and, after the week, checked them out.

Then I started doing trips to Cherry Hill, New Jersey,
where the bus would stay with you the whole week and
you'd go on different day trips—it's what they call a hub
and spoke trip. There were five day trips, and the group
would do Atlantic City one day, the race track and dinner
theaters on the following days. On other tours we did Niag-
ara Falls and the Thousand Islands.

Did you have any training?
Not really. I pretty much trained myself. Later I went to
ITMI, a tour management school in San Francisco. I
wanted to see how things were done at other companies
and how they trained tour directors. The school gave me a
different insight on the business.

**Would you recommend that kind of training before
looking for a job as tour director?**
It's definitely a plus. I really don't know if anybody would
hire somebody without training right out of high school in
today's market if he or she didn't at least have some experience.

What's your job like now?
I do several things. I set up tours for the company, which
means I go to a new destination and plan out an itinerary,
pick the attractions and the hotels to be used, price it out
and come up with a product to sell. I sell the tour to the
groups I deal with on a regular basis, and then I also go on

the trips and direct them to make sure everything goes well.

We go everywhere: Florida, Canada, Nova Scotia, Nashville, New Orleans, San Francisco, Lake Tahoe, Las Vegas, Hawaii, Alaska. Most of our tours are by motorcoach, but we sometimes fly to a destination and then do some touring by motorcoach or take cruises.

I work year-round for my company. We're very busy between May and October, but we also do some work in the off-season.

What do you like most about the job?
You're your own boss when you go out on the road. I have a lot of freedom to do what I want because I've been with the same company for over ten years.

I like not going to an office every day; I'm out there doing something new and different and learning all the time. And I like to meet all kinds of people. Of course, I like to travel. I start to get itchy if I haven't been on a trip for three or four weeks.

What don't you like?
The long hours and being on a time schedule. The effects on home life and social life are definitely a negative, especially if you're doing a lot of back-to-back trips. Fortunately, I can now pick which weeks I'm away.

What advice do you have for a would-be tour director?
You have to like to travel and be able to tolerate being away from home. It's fun, but there's a lot of responsibility when you're on the road, and you have to be able to handle it. You're in charge, and people depend on you to make sure everything goes smoothly. And you have to have a lot of common sense. When you're out there, there are a lot of decisions that are going to have to be made, from what time you're leaving in the morning to where you're going to stop for lunch and how long you're going to be on the bus.

What is the greatest benefit of being a tour director?
You get a lot of experience out there on the road, life experience that college can't give you. As a tour director you see the real world—the way other people live, even just in this country—and that's a great benefit.

Toby Marlow, 45,
tour guide/lecturer, Shortline Tours,
New York, New York
Years in travel: 17

How did you get into a career as tour guide?

Seventeen years ago, a friend of mine and I decided to open
our own local tour guide service and do private tours. I had
to get a tour guide license to give sightseeing tours. I took
the test, failed the first time and passed the second. Our
business never got off the ground, but I applied for a job
with Manhattan Sightseeing Tours.

The manager asked if I had a license, and I said, "Yes," so
he said, "Get on the bus." For two weeks straight, I got
aboard and listened to the guide, without pay. I made information cards for myself, and the man who trained me took
me under his wing. I probably walked in at the right time,
because it was March, before the company's busy season.

The job evolved year by year. I started out working part
time and went on unemployment when the season ended.
Things get quiet for at least two months right after Christmas. But I was able to get on the roster very soon and
started working full time.

Where do your tours go?

There are two basic bus tours, of upper and lower Manhattan. We go to the Statue of Liberty, the Empire State Building, the World Trade Center—all the famous places. The
tours last a few hours. Our passengers sign up for the tour
at their hotels and all meet in one spot.

Was it difficult starting out?

For me it was difficult because I wasn't very outgoing at
the time. A lot of our people have been in the theater, and
some have been teachers. I found it hard to stand in front
of people. The tough part is learning to project your voice
and remember what you need to say.

People want you to be entertaining, to smile and tell some
jokes, so in the beginning it can be stressful. The man who
was training me was very kind, and after practicing it began
to be more fun.

85

Do you like the job?

Most of the time I really like it. I like to show people this city. There's so much to see and tell the groups about. And most of the passengers are nice people. You kid around, joke with the bus driver, and everybody has a good time. I like the people I work with, and I have a good manager who cares about me and my family, which is very helpful. We don't have the travel benefits that other people in the travel industry might get. But my tour guide license has gotten me into attractions and museums and things all over the world free or at reduced rates, so that's an advantage.

Is there anything you don't like about the work?

Sometimes it's very tiring because there's a lot of walking and standing. And there's some pressure. You basically say the same things every day, so it looks really easy, but I'm exhausted at the end of the day. It can take a lot out of you because you're always dealing with groups of people, making sure they're happy, that they don't get lost or hurt. Things can happen to you or your group. Sometimes it's crime—people on my tour have been pickpocketed; another time my bag was taken right out of the bus in front of the office. And there are the other difficulties of working in a major city—pollution, noise, traffic, things like that.

What advice would you give someone considering becoming a city guide?

You have to be a pretty calm, easygoing person. You can't be rough and snappy or a wise guy kind of person because you'll turn people off. The business has gotten a lot tougher since I started too. Back then, all you needed was to be able to do the tour, give the information to the people, and that was sufficient. Now, sightseeing companies give training classes and are much more demanding about who they hire because there's more competition.

It's a good idea to have some travel experience. People like to share their experiences with you. They like to know that you've been places, especially places they've been to or lived in. And it helps you do the tour if you feel you understand them and have some sense of where they're from.

MORE INFORMATION PLEASE

The American Society of Travel Agents (ASTA)
1101 King Street
Alexandria, Virginia 22314
703-739-2782
    This organization can provide information about becoming a travel agent and about travel schools.

Future Airline Professionals Association
4959 Massachusetts Boulevard
Atlanta, Georgia 30337
800-JET-JOBS
    Write or call for a directory of domestic and international employers ($22).

Air Line Employees Association
5600 South Central Avenue
Chicago, Illinois 60638-3797
312-767-3333
    Write or call for a directory of training schools and educational programs and a monthly listing of job possibilities ($40 a year for both publications).

Association of Flight Attendants
1625 Massachusetts Avenue, NW #300
Washington, D.C. 20036
202-328-5400
    Write or call for a packet of information about working as a flight attendant.

Independent Federation of Flight Attendants
630 Third Avenue
New York, New York 10017
212-818-1130
    Write or call for information on finding a job as a flight attendant.

Air Transport Association of America
1709 New York Avenue, NW
Washington, D.C. 20006
202-626-4000
 Write or call for a directory of possible employers for airline reservations or customer service agent jobs.

Cruise Lines International Association
500 Fifth Avenue
New York, New York 10036
212-921-0066
 Write or call for a list of member cruise lines (for reservations or customer service agent jobs).

National Tour Association
546 E. Main Street
Lexington, Kentucky 40508
606-253-1036
 NTA's National Tour Foundation can help you find tour management internships.

WILL YOU FIT INTO THE WORLD OF TRAVEL?

Before you sign up for a program of study or start to look for one of the jobs described in this book, it's smart to figure out whether that career will be a good fit given your background, skills and personality. There are a number of ways to do that, including:

❑ Talk to people who already work in that field. Find out what they like and don't like about their jobs, what kinds of people their employers hire, and what their recommendations are about training. Ask them if there are any books or publications that would be helpful for you to read. Maybe you could even "shadow" the workers for a day as they go about their duties.

❑ Use a computer to help you identify career options. Some of the most widely used software programs are *Discover,* by the American College Testing Service; *SIGI Plus,* developed by the Educational Testing Service; and *Career Options,* by Peterson's. Some public libraries make this career software available to library users at little or no cost. The career counseling or guidance office of your high school or local community college is another possibility.

❑ Take a vocational interest test. The most common are the Strong-Campbell Interest Inventory and the Kuder Occupational Interest Survey. High schools

89

and colleges usually offer free testing to students and alumni at their guidance and career planning offices. Many career counselors in private practice or at community job centers can also give the test and interpret the results.

❏ Talk to a career counselor. You can find one by asking friends and colleagues if they know of any good ones. Or contact the career information office in the adult education division of a local college. Its staff and workshop leaders often do one-on-one counseling. The job information services division of major libraries sometimes offers low- or no-cost counseling by appointment. Or check the *Yellow Pages* under the heading "Vocational Guidance."

But first, before you spend time, energy or money doing any of the above, take one or more of the following five quizzes (one for each career discussed in the book). The results can help you evaluate whether you have the basic traits and abilities that are important to success in that career—in short, whether you are cut out for it.

If a career as a travel agent interests you, take this quiz:

Read each statement below, then choose the number 0, 5 or 10. The rating scale below explains what each number means.

> **0** = Disagree
> **5** = Agree somewhat
> **10** = Strongly agree

____I feel comfortable with computers and would be willing to learn more about using a computerized reservations system

____I have a good understanding of world geography

____I can handle several different kinds of tasks at the same time without losing track of details

____I am a good listener and know how to ask questions to get more information

___I am good at using research and reference materials quickly and accurately

___I can communicate information to others in a way that's easily understood

___I am persistent and don't mind the idea of making many phone calls to get an answer

___I wouldn't mind sitting at a desk eight hours a day

___I'm resourceful and can come up with new ideas and information when necessary

___I am patient with people who can't make up their minds or make decisions

Now add up your score.   ___Total points

If your total points are less than 50, you may want to reconsider your priorities or re-evaluate your suitability for a career as a travel agent. If your total points are between 50 and 75, you may have what it takes to be a good travel agent, but be sure to do more investigation. If your total points are 75 or more, it's likely that you have the interest and motivation to be a successful travel agent.

If a career as a flight attendant interests you, take this quiz:

Read each statement below, then choose the number 0, 5 or 10. The rating scale below explains what each number means.

$$0 = \text{Disagree}$$
$$5 = \text{Agree somewhat}$$
$$10 = \text{Strongly agree}$$

___I'm sensitive to other people's problems

___I've had work experience helping or serving people

___I'm good at solving problems quickly

___I have a knack for reassuring or calming my friends and co-workers

___Most people would describe me as warm and friendly

___There's nothing I like more than traveling

___I think I would react calmly and be able to give instructions to others in an emergency

___I am able to take charge in stressful situations

___I don't mind living away from my family and friends

___Even in difficult circumstances I keep my sense of humor

Now add up your score.   ___Total points

If you scored less than 50, then you probably do not have enough interest or experience in dealing with and serving the public to become a flight attendant. If your points totaled between 50 and 75, you may have the necessary personality qualities and interest in travel to become a flight attendant, but be sure to investigate the field further to decide if you have the experience and determination to land a job. If you scored over 75 points, consider yourself a prime candidate for securing a job as a flight attendant.

If a career as a reservations agent in the travel industry interests you, take this quiz:

Read each statement below, then choose the number 0, 5 or 10. The rating scale below explains what each number means.

0 = Disagree
5 = Agree somewhat
10 = Strongly agree

___I have some familiarity with computers and am willing to learn more about how to work on an automated reservations system

___I've had some experience selling products or services or working in a retail store

___I'm well spoken and use correct grammar in conversation

___I'm a very good listener; I understand and can remember what people tell me

___The idea of being on the phone eight hours a day doesn't bother me

___I can handle the pressure of making sales quotas

___Doing the same work every day in exchange for travel benefits is worthwhile to me

___I rarely lose my temper, even when dealing with difficult people

___I have a pleasant telephone voice

___Sitting at a desk all day long wouldn't be a problem for me

Now add up your score. ___Total points

If your total points are less than 50, you may not have the temperament or qualities you need to become a successful reservations agent. If your total points are between 50 and 75, you may have what it takes to work as a reservations agent, but be sure to do further evaluation before you apply for a job. If your total points are 75 or more, it's likely that a job as a reservations agent will be a good bet, given your interest in travel, your experience and your people skills.

If a career as a customer service agent in the travel industry interests you, take this quiz:

Read each statement below, then choose the number 0, 5 or 10. The rating scale below explains what each number means.

0 = Disagree
5 = Agree somewhat
10 = Strongly agree

___I think I have a good grasp of people's behavior and why they act the way they do

___I'm very good at making myself understood, even to strangers

___I'm good at soothing emotional people because I am a calm, even-tempered person

___I've noticed that people I don't know seem comfortable dealing with me from the start

___I enjoy solving problems and am good at figuring out what can be done

___No matter how rude strangers are to me, I don't take it personally

___I can usually see at least two sides to any argument

___I've had some experience dealing with the public

___I would like to work in an environment where travelers are coming and going

___For me, helping people or putting a smile on someone's face is very rewarding

Now add up your score.   ___Total points

If your total points were less than 50, you probably do not have enough interest or the right skills to solve travelers' problems. If you scored between 50 and 75 points, with further investigation and, perhaps, experience dealing with the public, you may do very well as a customer service agent. If your score was 75 points or more, you probably have the necessary skills, flair for problem solving and interest in helping people to be a first-rate customer service agent.

If you are interested in a career as a tour escort, take this quiz:

Read each statement below, then choose the number 0, 5 or 10. The rating scale below explains what each number means.

0 = Disagree
5 = Agree somewhat
10 = Strongly agree

___I am by nature a "counselor" type who has great patience for listening to and helping solve others' problems

___I can handle working long hours and days or even weeks without a day off

___I enjoy and am good at talking in front of groups

____I have the self-confidence to lead a group and rein in those who are creating problems

____I am very organized

____I am good at coming up with alternatives when plans fall through

____I like getting to know new people and am a good conversationalist

____I would enjoy doing library research to learn more about the history, culture and geography of a new place

____There's nothing more fun than traveling

____I don't mind being on my own and away from home for long periods

Now add up your score.   ____Total points

If your score added up to less than 50 points, chances are you are not cut out for working as a tour manager. If your total points were between 50 and 75, you probably have what it takes to pursue a career as a tour manager, but you may want to get some experience leading tours on a part-time or volunteer basis to find out for sure. If you scored above 75 points, you most likely have the experience and people skills to become a successful tour manager.

ABOUT THE AUTHOR

Robert F. Miller has written for and about the travel industry for many years while living in New York, western Massachusetts and Paris. He has covered the travel agency industry and the cruise business for travel trade publications and has written about travel for a variety of national magazines and newspapers. He also has contributed to or written a number of travel guides and other books.